∽ PRAISE FOR *Rebuild from Depression* ᶜ∽

"Oh, but you're not depressed? Every woman should read this book. Every pregnant woman will wish she had."

Nina Planck, author of
Real Food: What to Eat and Why

"*Rebuild from Depression* is going to be a very important book. Its dissection of the role of diet and nutrition is well-researched and an eye-opener. Medical science is beginning to give more value to the study of diet and particularly the role of nutrients in maintaining that delicate bodily balance called health.

It may be that increases in depression can be tied to our deteriorating eating habits in which "manufactured" food is progressively displacing "grown food." The medical community is trying to correct the ravages of diabetes, high blood pressure, and obesity and yet these diseases may represent the end-result of dietary manipulation by industry. We need to address the cause of these diseases: the food we are consuming is nutrient-shallow. *Rebuild from Depression* helps us do just that. Dr. Amanda Rose needs to be heard by the medical professionals as well as laymen."

Robert Kotler, MD, FACS
Clinical Instructor, UCLA
www.robertkotlermd.com

"In the arena of depression where the push is one pill fits all, it is refreshing to look at the holistic reality that depression has many stems and many causes. Depression really requires us to view this issue systemically, with care and honor for the client. Amanda Rose, in her fine book, reminds us of that need in an open, realistic discussion. I highly recommend this book for practitioners and their clients."

Gabrielle M. Guedet, PhD (Psychology)
Marriage and Family Therapist
Sacramento, California

"*Rebuild from Depression* provides real answers for reversing depression caused by common nutritional deficiencies. By giving you powerful information and practical steps to boost your awareness, it empowers you to live a happier, healthier life!"

Jan DeCourtney, CMT
Co-author, *Recapture Your Health*
www.sunrisehealthcoach.com

"Rebuild from Depression by Amanda G. Rose, PhD, is full of useful information for women, especially mothers and the people who support them. The author examines the ways in which the nutritional demands of pregnancy and the recovery period following childbirth can trigger postpartum depression, and often contribute to a lifelong depression. She presents a nutritional approach to providing protection against postpartum depression, and ideas for overcoming depression in women. As a doula, I'm looking forward to recommending this book to my clients."

Allison Coleman
Supporting Mom Services
Austin, Texas

"In my work at the Alta Bates Summit Medical Center in Oakland I deal with grief every day and with its cousin, depression. We all need survival tools to help us get through tough times. Rose's book, *Rebuild from Depression,* gives us depression-fighting tools to last a lifetime."

Patricia Broemmel, MA
(Bioethics / Theology) Hospital Chaplain,
Berkeley, California

"Two years ago this week I was detained by the state of California and sent to a mental hospital for a 72 hour evaluation after a visit to the ER. I had not slept and barely eaten in 7 days. I was sure that God was going to take me home and that I would die in the institution. My baby was 9 weeks old. I turned a major corner about 3 weeks ago after about 6 intense weeks of nutritional supplements, amino acids, and traditional foods. I am convinced that rebuilding through nutrition will cure me.

I am a skeptic about "cures" in general. When Amanda used to tell me about depression and nutrition, I just did not get it. I thought that I inherited mental illness from my father's side and there was nothing I could do besides accept it and take medications. Then one day, by the grace of God, a lightbulb went on and it all made sense. I am on the path to wellness now, as I call it. Knowing also that Amanda is well, and she had mental illness in her family, made me rethink my whole paradigm about mental illness.

My B-6 and zinc levels are already increasing after 2.5 months. I had severe anemia and someone who I had not seen in a few months looked at me and said, "You have color in your face, my dear!"

It is never too late for you to get well and influence the generations to come."

Jennifer S., mother of two,
27 years old, California

"How enlightening! Dr. Rose's personal story is inspiring, and her advice for how I can take action in my own struggle with vitamin deficiencies is empowering. I highly recommend her book for all women whether they are simply hoping to be mothers in the future or are struggling to regain their mental and physical health from past pregnancies."

Lindsay Rhein, mother of two

"Amanda Rose, PhD, has packed an amazing amount of useable information into this must-read book. It not only addresses *why* people can suffer from depression, but also *how* one can fix it. Thanks to Amanda, I have learned to love liver."

Youngiee Quennell
Oregon

"Wow! I've ignored all responsibilities in my life (other than my daughter and the dog) over the last five days because I've spent every spare minute my daughter was asleep reading *Rebuild from Depression*. From my own similar journey, I do believe that God wants us to be healthy and to thrive on the foods He gave us instead trying to improve on what He has made perfectly. This book will lead people to this truth and in the right direction."

Moneca Dunham

"Amanda's book, *Rebuild from Depression*, have inspired me to find a nutritional solution to my depression. I have used homeopathy and nutritional supplements instead of the antidepressants that I was on previously. Her well-researched, informative book, along with her story, can help when looking for the root cause of depression. Her troubleshooting lists really help one to know where to begin to seek help for nutritional support. And her recipes are great, too!"

Jennifer

REBUILD FROM DEPRESSION

REBUILD FROM DEPRESSION

A NUTRIENT GUIDE

including

DEPRESSION IN PREGNANCY AND POSTPARTUM

Amanda Rose, PhD

with
Annell Adams, MD

Purple Oak Press
P.O. Box 37
California Hot Springs, California 93207
www.PurpleOakPress.com

This book contains many details concerning food nutrients and depression. Although great care was taken to ensure the accuracy of the text, all individuals have unique medical needs and should seek advice from a qualified health professional. This book is a resource on food nutrients, not a substitute for medical treatment. The authors and the publisher are not engaged in medical treatment and are not providing medical advice to individual readers. The authors and the publisher shall not be held liable for any harm or loss purported to arise, directly or indirectly, from any information in this book.

ISBN: 978-1-934712-10-8
First U.S. Edition, 2009

Cover and interior designed by Sterling Hill Productions.

Purple Oak Press
P.O. Box 37
California Hot Springs, CA 93207
www.purpleoakpress.com

CONTENTS

*M*y grandmother died at the age of sixty-one of complications from postpartum depression. I know it sounds crazy. She had postpartum depression back in the 1940s and 1950s, before the condition had a name. She was institutionalized twice after "nervous breakdowns," was given what my granddad called her "I-don't-give-a-shit pills," and had shock therapy when those pills were not sufficient.

The shock therapy helped her return to her family and function at a basic level, perhaps because it raised her brain levels of zinc. She normally displayed signs of zinc deficiencies—her very small frame in a family of larger people is one indicator, and as she proceeded through life she developed other diseases in addition to depression, that are associated with low zinc, magnesium, B vitamins, and Omega-3 fatty acids. She developed type 1 diabetes at the age of fifty and she died at the age of sixty-one "with the heart of an eighty-year-old," according to her cardiologist.

When I've spoken with women and tell them about my grandmother's death from postpartum depression at sixty-one, they don't think I'm crazy at all. Their eyes widen and they say, "My problems started after I had my children." Diabetes, thyroid disease, chronic fatigue syndrome, rheumatoid arthritis, fibromyalgia, and cardiac problems top the list of diseases that these women in my life report to me.

As women experience degenerative diseases that appear rooted in their postpartum days or in another very difficult period in their lives, researchers are finding that some diseases are not only correlated with each other, but that they share common nutritional deficiencies. Depression, heart disease, and diabetes are good examples. If you have one of these diseases you are likely to have another or to develop another in the future. There is growing research that increasing Omega-3 fatty acids in the diet or taking a supplement can alleviate all three.

It seems no coincidence to me that my grandmother, who produced three children, each of whom needed her Omega-3 fatty acids for their developing brain, developed diseases related to Omega-3 fatty acid deficiency. She had no idea that her diet was not sufficient to grow three children without health consequences for herself.

In this context, my grandmother gave up a great deal for her children. Her husband of all those years is still alive, in his late eighties, and he has only given up his golf game in the last few months. He was able to keep his nutrient stores to himself all those years. For my grandmother's part, we have celebrated the twenty-fifth anniversary of her death by publishing this book.

The World Health Organization (WHO) has a term for these "lost years" of my grandmother's life—disability adjusted life years, or DALYs. These are the years of life lost due to early death or disability. I argue that my grandmother's years lost to early death may be twenty-five, though it is surely hard to know how long she would have lived had she been healthy. Her sisters lived high-quality lives past the age of ninety.

But on top of her early death, she lost many more years due to disability caused by depression. From all reports, many of her years between her early twenties and her death at sixty-one were lost due to disability from depression and its complications. She may have lost closer to sixty-five years of life from both early death and from health-related disabilities.

Among women in industrialized countries, depression is now the number one cause of DALYs according to the WHO. I have lost at least three years myself and I am fairly young and have not been plagued by lifelong depression. I am lucky in this regard.

However, the outlook for babies born now is not good. When my son, Frederick, is twenty-eight years old in 2030, the WHO projects that depression will be the second-greatest cause of lost years of life due to early death or disability, *for men and women across the globe*. All those years of depressive hell or a life cut short by suicide will add up. And for the population on this planet, those years lost due to depression will be second only to those lost due to HIV/AIDS.

Years lost due to other diseases will decline and our struggles with depression will continue unchecked. Our children will be affected by debilitating depression and suicide if the WHO forecast is correct. And our generation, too, will continue to be plagued by the disease if trends continue as they have.

Tools to Change the Trends

In this day, none of us should suffer from a lack of nutrients, and yet studies show that providing patients with vitamin B-12 or folic acid alleviates depression. Surveys of the food intake of American women show that many of us do not eat adequate quantities of folate, magnesium, zinc, B-6, and Omega-3 fatty acids. All these nutrients (and many others) can cause or aggravate depression if we do not consume enough of them.

How do we know which nutrients will help us fight depression?

I started the research for this book because I wanted to rebuild from depression myself. I felt as if I was in a continuous game of "pin the tail on the donkey." I was blindfolded, searching for that paper donkey on the wall, and hoping to pin the tail on the donkey's hind end. One more supplement would do it. One more diet change would work. The proverbial tail would end up in the right place and I would feel well again.

I played "pin the tail on the donkey" until my thyroid became sluggish and I gained fifty pounds. Like the many diseases my grandmother faced postpartum, I now had a thyroid problem—and no pants that fit. I headed to the library and collected the information in this book.

How do we know if we need to eat more of a particular nutrient? What is the best test for deficiency? How can we add it to our bodies with nutritional supplements? What is the best kind of supplement? How much is too much? How do we increase our food intake of nutrients or our body's absorption of them? This book answers these questions.

The answers to these questions will cut the time you spend playing "pin the tail on the donkey" and you, too, will rebuild from depression. As we rebuild, we will change the current depression trends.

If we do nothing, our children are likely to suffer from depression and we will continue to suffer over the remaining decades of our lives. Whatever are the underlying causes of each of our unique cases of depression, our children are likely to share some of those same characteristics. It is a matter of basic biology that along with our eye color and hair color, we also give our babies our nutritional status. After creating them, they share food with us at the dinner table for many years.

Those same deficiencies that are wreaking havoc in our bodies now are likely to do so in our children and in their children until the cycle is broken. If we can break the cycle, we will have a better quality of life. We can help our children with theirs, and we can affect the trend lines in depression forecasts.

The second part of this book on nutrients and food offers strategies to maximize the nutrition in your diet. These strategies, implemented over time on days that you feel well, will help you shore up your body. You can gain some inspiration from knowing that not only will your quality of life improve, but you will be giving your children important tools to improve their quality of life. They are not destined to be depressed and your destiny is not fixed either.

We will rebuild from depression. The tools are waiting for us. Use them at a pace you can manage, but begin to implement them. Help your family members and friends implement them. In 2030, rather than lament the global rise in depression, we will celebrate the impact we have made on our own lives and on the lives of those around us.

~◦ 1 ◦~

Pre-Pregnancy to Birth

I grew up relatively underprivileged and enjoyed very inexpensive and fresh-from-the-garden dinners of pinto beans, brown rice with butter, and vegetables. We ate eggs from our own flock of Rhode Island Red hens and had occasional milk from a friend's goat. The butter was my mother's biggest extravagance and, save the year or so around the fifth grade where I lived on peanut butter and honey, butter and eggs were my primary source of fat in those formative days of my life. My primary sources of protein were pinto beans, brown rice, butter, eggs, and tuna, as well as the unknown number of insects that made their way onto my salad plate. It is one of my fond memories that as I finished my salad one evening, I noticed a tiny, translucent snail making its way across the plate in my salad dressing. Surely I ate countless others.

Despite the good beginnings on the organic garden diet, I cut my food intake drastically as a teenager and into my twenties, in my efforts to have a body worthy of the California image.

In late high school through college, and into graduate school, I joined the low-fat diet craze and lived on 10 grams of fat a day (or even less when I was highly motivated to lose weight). The only fat to enter my diet was small amounts of chicken fat, and even the chicken was limited in my nearly all-vegetarian diet. I ate many "fat-free" products, most memorably some sort of cheese substitute with each slice wrapped in its own plastic. I added that cheese to fat-free bread regularly for sandwiches.

Of course, none of those dietary choices was effective in the long-term fat battle and I do blame dieting throughout my teens and twenties as one of the primary culprits in this story I am telling.

Measuring Up

As if yo-yo dieting was not bad enough, I put myself under a great deal of pressure beginning in college. I had grown up in an impoverished town in central California; Delano, home of the United Farm Workers. Delano is not the poorest town in the state, but close to it. My father actually grew up in a community that is arguably the poorest in the state, a community just 10 miles north of Delano called Teviston.

You will not likely find Teviston on any map but it is located about forty-five minutes north of Bakersfield in the San Joaquin Valley of California. Teviston was settled in the 1930s and was one of the few areas in the state in the 1930s and early 1940s where African-Americans could buy land. When my dad retired in the late 1990s, one of his colleagues who grew up in Teviston credited the Rose Family with "bringing color to Teviston"—our family was the only white family in a community of African-Americans.

My grandparents were among the better-off portion of the small Teviston community because they owned a few acres and a small house built by my great-grandpa. They were able to retire on their social security income after years of field work and truck driving. My own grandpa added on the bathroom some years later and covered over the outhouse hole. The shower—also built by my grandpa—was highly funky, with exposed plumbing in the ceiling.

We had Thanksgiving and Christmas dinners in my grandpa's workshop, set up with a wooden picnic table covered by a vinyl tablecloth and heated with a woodstove handmade from a barrel. I never considered that this lifestyle was not normal. When my husband visited my grandma years later, he was shocked by their housing. He had never seen such poverty—and of course they were one of the better-off families in the area.

In this context, I decided to attend college at Santa Clara University, a Jesuit college in the San Francisco Bay Area of California. Santa Clara tends to attract students from very wealthy families. The difference in wealth between my upbringing and most of the Santa Clara population was not such a problem for me, but I also perceived that I would not be able to perform well in college compared to these other students who had many more opportunities. I did have a good high school transcript, but I was not ignorant about the differences in education programs across communities. I knew my education was likely quite inferior.

No one told me that pretty much everybody who is accepted to Santa Clara actually does finish. I worked my tail off, stressed that I would not make it, and I did graduate just like everyone else. After graduation, like a glutton for punishment, I went on to graduate school in political science. Friends in graduate school got ulcers. I had no such obvious signs that stress was eating away at my body, though I did manage to part with my gallbladder in those years.

In those graduate school days, I got married, and my husband and I each acquired the other's bad habits. Before marriage, I rarely exercised and my husband Sander lived on boxes of macaroni and cheese, but I did watch my diet by eating low-fat food and Sander did exercise a great deal. In marital bliss, together we did not exercise nor did we watch what we ate. We remained hydrated on coffee and at least one 32-ounce soda a day from a local haunt (for the low cost of thirty-five cents). We did maintain our commitment to the environment, however, by reusing our Styrofoam cups from those thirty-five-cent sodas.

We ate often at a cheap Chinese restaurant and typically ordered the General's Chicken meal. The chicken was batter fried and smothered in sweet and sour sauce. The meal was rounded off with greasy fried rice and extra-crispy egg rolls.

During one summer, Borders Cafe introduced its fantastic "Mocha Freeze" and we had a promotional sample, lamenting about how we could not afford such a treat regularly at the price of more than three dollars a drink.

I then had the bright idea of how to make a "Mocha Freeze" at home ourselves. It was very simple:

1) Make a pot of coffee and sweeten the coffee when hot, with lots of sugar.
2) Cool the coffee in the refrigerator.
3) Make coffee ice cubes with a portion of the cold coffee.

4) Buy chocolate syrup, whole milk, and whipped cream in a can.

5) In a blender, mix the chilled coffee, several coffee ice cubes, chocolate syrup, and milk.

6) Pour into a large glass and spray whipped cream on top.

Try this at home if you wish. It is good for gaining about 10 pounds over the course of a summer.

Even Sander, who can just about eat anything and maintain his weight, got pretty chunky.

My husband Sander decided to hit the road, leave graduate school behind sometime in our fifth year, and find a private sector job in Michigan.

A good friend of ours said, "When you're in the middle of a big move, that's the time to make changes in your life. Everything is changing anyway, your changes won't be as noticeable."

So I did it: I decided that I would not allow myself to drink soda in the state of Michigan. This was the first of the many "structural reforms" I would impose on myself to help me regain my health. On trips or holidays outside of Michigan, I could have a soda, but never in Michigan.

Within two months of the move, a good friend of ours died at a young age of asthma, a condition worsened by her diet choices. In that same time period, I happened upon an article about breast cancer and trans-fatty acids—that diets high in trans-fatty acids (partially hydrogenated oils found in most processed foods) were associated positively with breast cancer. I knew my diet was poor and all the cheap Chinese food in Bloomington surely did not help my breast cancer risk. I started immediately on a weight loss diet, cut out the bad fats, and shifted towards a diet very low in animal products.

During those dieting days in Michigan I spent about an hour each day at the gym lifting weights and doing cardiovascular exercises, I improved my diet, and I ate a lot less food. On a typical day I drank one soy-based protein shake made with soy powder, soy milk, and a piece of fruit. I ate one main meal in about the middle of the afternoon that was protein-centered with a fresh vegetable. I learned to cook tofu quite well in that time and often prepared tofu-centered dishes. We also ate salmon at home or at sushi restaurants two times a week because of its high Omega-3 content. In the fall of 1997, I entered my Michigan apartment wearing a large size 20. By early spring when all the neighbors came outdoors to defrost themselves from the Michigan winter, one of my neighbors did not recognize me. I was a large size 14 at that point, I had lost 40 to 50 pounds, and I felt great.

We moved to California in May of 1998 to start a data analysis and consulting business. I continued a near-vegan diet in which the only animal products I consumed were salmon about twice a week and occasionally honey. I added olive oil and flax seeds to my foods regularly to increase my consumption of beneficial oils. I consumed nutritional yeast as well to help with my energy and my B vitamin levels. My primary protein in those years came from soy beans and other legumes. My soy protein sources were tofu, soy milk, soy protein powder, and occasionally tempeh.

At this point in my life I was very health conscious. We made a strong effort to eat only whole foods, save the occasional soy protein shake I would drink a few times a week or a meal bar I would eat when I needed a quick food fix. We decided it was time to have a baby late in 2000, so I became extra-diligent about my diet. I even spoke to a doctor about what I should be doing to prepare for conception. He implied that I was a bit obsessed and asked what I would do if I ended up outliving everyone. I figured we were ready for a baby.

It took us about eight months to conceive Frederick and in those months I was militant about being healthy. On top of the diet, I exercised regularly. In fact, on the day before I found out I was pregnant, I leg-pressed 325 pounds at the gym. It was my goal for about six months before that day to press 300 pounds. I was so disgusted with a negative pregnancy test I had received two days before, I put my energy into my legs and shocked a number of weight lifters at the gym. There were not many women in the gym who could do a full set of leg presses at 325 pounds and certainly none who were chunky like me.

I entered my pregnancy physically strong and, theoretically, nutritionally sound from my diet and lifestyle diligence.

Pregnancy

On August 18, 2001, I found out I was pregnant. On August 19, I began to feel exhausted. My sister was married one week later and I was able to contribute to decorating and setup but at a much dialed-down rate. When we returned from the wedding in late August, at just over five weeks pregnant, I could not get off the couch. I spent days on the couch with the energy to do absolutely nothing. I did not shop for groceries. I did not prepare meals. I did not move garden hoses. It is no exaggeration to say that I did nothing in those days.

Those peak exhaustion days lasted until September 22, when I was nine weeks pregnant, the day of the wedding of a family friend. My husband had purchased the wedding present and it was my job to gift wrap it. I looked at the stash of wrapping paper we had and decided we had none appropriate. I wondered if I could make the trip to the store by car, about five blocks away. It was morning and I had a little bit of energy but I was concerned about saving my energy for the wedding that evening. I decided to risk the trip.

I arrived at the store to discover that the gift wrap was $5 for a small roll. I was shocked at the price and thought I should go to a discount store instead. I remember staring at the gift wrap, contemplating the short drive to the discount store. I would have to drive there, get out of my car, walk across the hot parking lot, find gift wrap, stand in line, pay for it, walk across the hot parking lot again, get into the now hot car, and drive home. I was concerned that I would have to call home for help. I didn't have a cell phone, so just finding a pay phone might be more than I could handle. I still had a bit of energy and decided to take the risk. I did it. I bought four rolls of gift wrap (some of which we still have) and returned home to wrap the wedding present.

We went to the wedding that evening and, contrary to expectations, I made it through the wedding and into the reception before needing to go home. It was the first day since late August that I did anything but lay on that couch.

After that day, I had about one good energy day for about every five days on the couch. On the good days I could do regular light housework or some of my data analysis. On the bad days, I laid on the couch.

By October 6, 2001, the date of another friend's wedding, I had one good day for every four bad days. But even those good days were hard. Sometime just before the wedding, my friend met me at the mall to help me pick out some bigger clothes for my expanding body. The first sign that I was not doing well should have been that, with her encouragement, I bought a pair of bright purple pants. This particular friend is tall, slim, and has a lot of flair. She can get away with such a fashion statement, but not all of us can.

We continued our shopping and I found myself sitting in a dressing room unable to move. I rested while she modeled some clothes for me. When she was ready, I made my way to the cash register. I leaned on the cash register counter as she bought her items, trying to maintain my balance and recover some energy. I did not think I was doing that poorly, but the clerk nearly called an ambulance. I could not have looked very good. That day at the mall was a "good" one since I had the energy to leave the house.

At the end of the first trimester in late October, I remember feeling cheated that I was not feeling any better. Weren't you supposed to get your energy back, magically, when you cross that threshold from twelve weeks to thirteen weeks pregnant? Even my good days were still relatively bad. Nothing at all magical happened as I entered the second trimester.

I did not have normal energy until I was twenty-one weeks pregnant and the energy lasted for four weeks. In those weeks, I sewed curtains and table linens and I pruned trees and shrubs in the yard, activities I knew I would not have time for once baby arrived. We had a wonderful New Year's Eve in that time and I felt rather normal, albeit pregnant.

DEPRESSION HITS

The signs of depression had begun in those days of fatigue, though I did not recognize them at the time. At about eighteen weeks pregnant, it was time to schedule the twenty-week ultrasound. My midwife suggested that we do the ultrasound at twenty-two weeks since I was so fat. Well, she might not have said it that way exactly, but that is my memory and I was very hurt and considered finding another midwife. My level of emotional sensitivity should have been a warning sign for us. It would not be long before the crash.

At the same appointment I found out that I had gained eight pounds in the previous month even though I was watching my eating and exercising regularly. I obsessed over my weight in those weeks in a way I had not in a long time. I was a size 14, so I had been a lot larger in my life, but the obsession remained. I did not stop eating or begin exercising incessantly, but I began to do things like take pictures of my growing belly and obsess about whether I had too much fat on my belly for ultrasound waves to penetrate. Such a level of obsession and anxiety is associated with depression as well.

I mentioned the situation to the other midwife in the practice who was more overweight than I and she rolled her eyes. Commiseration always helps. But when I did not gain any weight at the time of the next checkup after my 8-pound gain in the previous month, she thought I had gone on a dysfunctional diet, though she did not say so directly. She scheduled another ultrasound to make sure the baby was developing properly.

I resisted the ultrasound and said, "So what will we do if baby is not developing properly? If there is nothing we can do, I don't see the need for an ultrasound." She said, "You will have to spare your energy by going on bed rest and start on a higher calorie diet." Her message to me in my compromised brain was loud and clear: I am starving the baby because I am concerned about my weight gain. I considered canceling the appointment, but was already scared that my baby was not developing properly. It was early January.

By about January 10, the depression hit with a vengeance. I had never had serious depression before so I did not recognize it right away. I just thought everyone was trying to drive me crazy. I had two situations with clients that were getting out of hand. Employees of two of the clients had their own needs for therapy and were acting out to some degree. The situation was nothing that you do not find all the time, in every workplace, but I could not deal with it. I felt like I was being abused. I felt needled constantly by every communication with these people. In one case I finally broke down and threatened the person that I would go to his board in my pregnant state to report that he was attempting to increase the rate of premature births in the county. In this particular case, the premature birth rate was one of the outcomes they were trying to reduce. He responded in a bit of a panic.

One morning in early February, exhausted by the world that was driving me crazy, I found myself in the backyard sobbing uncontrollably. I tried to garden to keep up my spirits but then burst into uncontrollable sobs. I regained control for a moment only to begin sobbing again.

Before the sobbing began, I had phoned my mother who was about an hour away at the time. She could hear in my voice that something was wrong and knew that my husband Sander was gone for the day. She told me that she would drive down in a few hours to spend the day with me.

My mom found me red-faced and trying to control myself. There was nothing apparent that precipitated the sobbing. It just happened. My mom said to me, "Mandy, I came here today because I want you to know that I care about you. I don't know if you need me here today and if you don't, I'll go, but you should know that I will stay as long as need be."

My mom would eventually move in and then buy a house across the street, but in the short term we decided that I needed medication for my depression.

MEDICATION

The depression was severe at this point in my pregnancy, about 30 weeks in. We decided that medication was the only recourse. Sander and I went to the midwife and I said, "I need medication. My depression is out of control."

"Have you tried diet and exercise?" she asked.

I expect I gave her a very dirty look. "Of course I have tried all that stuff—I've done it all by the book, I'm miserable, and I need help."

I really did look fine. I am sure that the midwife assumed that my depression was fairly minor and that exercise would help take the edge off of it.

"Have you had thoughts of suicide?" she asked.

"Yes, passing thoughts, but I don't think I could kill the baby and I don't know how I'd take myself out alone," I said in a matter-of-fact tone.

What I said was true but I figured that since I could not kill myself without injuring the baby that I was pretty safe from the threat of suicide.

The midwife thought differently. "Here is a starter kit," she said. The kit was a freebie provided by the pharmaceutical company in a very nice package. She described how to take the medication and to work my way up to a full dose each day. The package provided different dosage levels so that I could work my way up to my full dose. It also provided a nice illustration of the problem of stopping the medication immediately. The midwife told me that once I start feeling good I might be tempted to stop taking the medication, but that my good feelings would likely be the result of the medication so I should continue on the medication through the pregnancy. And, like the kit, she emphasized the need to wean off of the medication rather than stop abruptly. I felt very educated.

Though I saw no other recourse but to medicate myself, I asked, "Will the medication affect the baby?"

She said, "Depression will affect the baby."

We left with drug in hand.

Sander and I went out to lunch and happened to bring the starter kit in with us. The starter kit sat there like another guest at the table. We stared at it. I handled it a number of times. Sander handled it and read the packaging.

Patients should be advised to notify their physician if they are pregnant
or intend to become pregnant during therapy.
Patients should be advised to notify their physician if they are
breastfeeding an infant.

We had agreed the night before that there was no other way. Medication was the only alternative. But the comment of the midwife in response to my question, "will the medication affect the baby?" played in my head. The statement "depression will affect the baby" is a bit cagey.

"What kind of response is *that*?" I wondered. I asked Sander. We both became suspicious.

Throughout that lunch as we read the label on the starter kit and the warnings, we began to get cold feet and both agreed that we should do a quick Internet search on the medication just to make sure we were not making any bad decisions.

We found out that antidepressants are a "category C" drug, which means either (1) animal studies have shown adverse effects and there are no well-controlled studies in pregnant women or (2) no animal studies have been conducted and there are no well-controlled studies in pregnant women. This particular medication was a category C drug for the first reason. I had been so diligent in my diet, I had not taken a Tylenol during the whole pregnancy, and in fact, Sander did not let me put gas in the car during the entire pregnancy because of the danger posed by the fumes. We sure are an obsessive pair! Now we were facing a category C drug that I would be taking every day. We were suddenly at a loss because I needed help, but we did not feel good about the medication option.

We turned to our next door neighbors, both therapists, to ask about this issue. They did express concern about the effect of the medication on the baby. They further suggested that it would be terrible to go through the birth process itself medicated. "You want to be able to enjoy the birth experience. You may well be a zombie with this medication."

They suggested that I look for solutions that would put off medication through the birth. They recommended that I see a homeopath that they used for asthma; a homeopathic remedy might take the edge off of the depression.

HOMEOPATHY

The family practice doctor I visited to discuss all my preconception planning is also a classical homeopath. The homeopath ran down a list of questions about preferences, tastes, and habits and was able to fit me into a homeopathic "type" and provide me with a remedy. My remedy was calcium carbonate and it did actually seem to work. When I was taking the remedy regularly, it took the edge off of the depression and it helped me get through until the delivery.

STRUCTURES

One of the biggest problems I was having in this period was dealing with other people, so we decided to reduce my people contact in order to reduce the amount of stress I was under. I did not answer the phone under any circumstances. I did not check my e-mail. Since I was still working in the business, Sander would read all of my business e-mails and screen them for me.

"Amanda, this is an e-mail from Susan and she is just wondering about the parent data."

Had Sander not screened my e-mail, I would have sat frozen at my computer desk, looking at my inbox, worrying about what lurked in each message. I may have avoided some messages for days, worrying about their content.

The same was true with the telephone: I would panic just at the sound of the phone ringing. For the few moments it took for me to walk to the phone and answer it, I would face incredible dread about what message waited for me on the other end.

On September 11, 2001, about seven weeks into the pregnancy, I stopped reading all newspapers and listening to news broadcasts. For nearly three years from September of 2001, the only news I watched was the 2002 election returns. For a person with a PhD in political science and a background in voting and elections, this was a huge behavioral shift. I got a call from a pollster during a primary election in one of my "up swings" when I was answering the phone. I always love answering phone surveys. The surveyor asked if I planned on voting in the March election. I was stunned because I did not realize there was an election. "Um, I'm not sure." "Thank you, ma'am." End of survey.

I reduced my workload as well. Less work meant fewer calls, fewer e-mails, and fewer meetings. I could still do the analysis itself, but I could not manage to work with people. These key structural changes allowed me to survive for the eight additional weeks of my pregnancy.

Throughout most of my pregnancy I was able to continue my exercise program, though I reduced the amount of weight I was lifting. I also began craving dairy products at about twenty weeks and ate a good deal of cottage cheese in the pregnancy, even though dairy had been off my diet for some time. I added some meat to my diet later after becoming concerned about taking in enough protein.

~⊃ 2 ⊂~

Birth

*A*t about the time I started on my homeopathic treatment, I began to wonder when the baby would turn from the breech position. At each appointment I asked expectantly, "Has the baby turned yet?"

Perhaps there is something to the "law of attraction" and we attract what we think about. Baby was breech for the entire pregnancy.

At about 37 ½ weeks my midwife explained that baby was breech and we needed to schedule a C-section. I was mortified.

In those last two weeks of the pregnancy, I used all the home methods I could to turn the baby, but to no avail. My favorite remedy was using our ironing board as a "slant board." I leaned it up against a table at about a forty-five-degree angle, lay on it for about ten minutes, and then immediately rolled off in an effort to turn the baby.

The baby did not turn, but some weeks after the birth I overheard my mom and Sander talking about the ironing board.

"It looks like it was run over by a truck," Sander exclaimed.

"What in the world happened to that?" my mom chimed in.

"That was my slant board and it didn't work," I called out from another room.

My slant board did nothing but damage the ironing board. I recommend one of those antique ironing boards if you are going to take this approach. Their construction is much more sound.

At thirty-eight weeks, I was depressed, in no shape to advocate for myself, and in no shape to find a person who could do a breech delivery. I called a local acupuncturist who laughed over the phone about turning a breech baby so late in pregnancy.

Faced with a breech baby and scheduled C-section, I struggled in those last days of pregnancy. I had a very calm exterior but I was fighting demons. I panicked that I would be giving birth to some decrepit creature. I tried to remind myself that I had an ultrasound that showed a baby growing in my womb, not a freak of nature. If I had a developing monster inside of me, surely the ultrasound would have shown some evidence. The ultrasound showed arms and legs and hands and feet and a face. All major human organs were present and accounted for. The medical evidence that I was growing a baby was pretty convincing.

But I was not rational, not inside my head in those last days. I had to talk myself down from worrying about this monster I was birthing. I just kept telling myself that I would love the baby regardless of what he or she (or it) looked like.

Negative thoughts of the baby, thoughts of my own death, and concerns over the baby's health filled my head. In a healthy mental state, these thoughts would have been fleeting if I had thought them at all. In a state of depression, the thoughts plagued me like they do many women. I could not turn them off. My anxiety over the birth increased. My obsession over details increased as I tried to control anything at all in my life and keep all those bad thoughts from coming about.

BIRTHDAY

On the day of the birth, I drove us to the hospital and checked myself into my room. I was prepped for surgery and wheeled down to the surgical area. Soon my midwife showed up and I knew that the time was near. She was very supportive and held my body very still while the anesthesiologist inserted the needle into my spine. I felt a sharp pinch. The anesthesiologist stayed to monitor me and she made small talk. The surgery began.

Sander had joined us just before the cutting started. He was at my head with a camera. The anesthesiologist was to my left. My arms were stretched out at my sides on arm rests. A sheet blocked my view of my abdominal region and of my midwife who was assisting the surgeon on the other side of the sheet. The anesthesiologist kept her hand on my left arm, I am sure both to provide me comfort and to continue to monitor me. I felt no pain. In fact, I felt nothing at all in the lower section of my body except some tugging.

Soon my midwife said, "Sander, you better get the camera ready."

The sheet dropped, Sander snapped the photo, and the anesthesiologist exclaimed excitedly, "You have a beautiful baby boy!"

I was amazed. I had a human baby.

Sander joined the baby across the room. Baby cried and cried.

The nurse brought baby to my side for a quick look-see before whisking him off to weigh and measure him. I remember the surprise and delight I felt when I saw baby for the first time and realized that not only did I have a humanoid baby, but that I had the most beautiful baby in the world. He was swaddled in a plaid hospital blanket and had a little knit hat on. His eyes were closed and he had stopped crying once he was swaddled. He looked content and perfect.

I had been told I would get to hold him at this point but the nurse just showed him to me and whisked him away. I knew that I would be able to hold him in the recovery room so I focused on getting through the surgery. As I was being stitched up, I had the sudden sensation that I was no longer human. The spinal medication was affecting my body; it did not feel like my body at all. A strange numbness overtook me and I began to get shaky. I fought an odd sort of nausea that I have never experienced before. I began to panic that I would never recover. It took all my energy to relax my mind and my body and pray that I would make it into the recovery room. I kept my thoughts on being rolled into the recovery room where I would get to hold and nurse my baby.

I was wheeled into recovery and waited for my baby. The recovery nurse monitored my vital signs and I continued to pray that I would feel human again. Slowly, I began to improve. Some minutes passed before I had the energy to ask about my baby. The recovery nurse did not answer.

The midwife came in. I said, "You said I would have the baby in the recovery room, where is he?" She left to investigate and returned to say, "He is bundled up under a heater and he is soooo cute." I felt betrayed again: I should be his heater. He should be on *my* chest, not in a warming drawer. I kept asking about him.

Finally someone sent in Sander to report to me.

"Baby is having breathing problems. They are assessing his lungs and need to observe him for a little longer. Are you OK?"

"Sander, please stay with our baby. I don't want him to be alone. I will be OK."

Sander left and I was pronounced recovered and ready to return to my room, but there was no nurse to take me there. There was a shift change at that time and not enough nurses in surgery to wheel my gurney to the elevator and up to my room. I heard the nurse in surgery negotiating with nurses from my wing: "OK, we can provide one person to take her up but you need to send someone down here. She's out of recovery now." Another woman was being wheeled out from her surgery and into the recovery room. The recovery room had room for one and I was crowding the place.

I was wheeled into the hallway and I was told that the nurses would be there right away to wheel me to my room. I lay on the gurney watching for signs of Sander and our baby. They were coming with me and I did not want them to get lost. Doors opened and closed.

A woman was rolled into the surgery room. "Do you know that if you have your tubes tied that you will never be able to have children again? Are you sure you want that?" She was quite sure and she was wheeled from the hallway into the surgery room.

The hallway was empty except for me and my gurney. I lay there and could only move my arms and crane my neck. I could hear shuffling in other rooms. Several times a door opened and I would crane my head expectantly, watching for Sander and the baby. A minute or two passed and each minute felt like an hour as I waited alone in the hallway on the gurney, unable to move. I have never felt such deep loneliness.

The nurses coordinated their efforts and found me in the hallway. They began to move me.

I said, "Wait, my baby is coming too, I don't want him to get lost."

One nurse assured me, "They know where to find you. We need to get you to your room now."

Once in my room I began talking to the nurse about my baby.

"My baby will be here any minute, I need to get ready."

She looked at me intently and said, "I work in the NICU a lot, let me check this out."

She made the call and then explained to me that my baby had a lung disorder called pneumothorax where air leaks out through the holes in the

---

Seek Treatment Today for Depression in Pregnancy
Annell Adams, MD.

Historically, pregnancy was thought to be protective. The myth of a blissful expectant period filled with joy and images of content, plump babies nursing at the breast pervade our cultural beliefs surrounding pregnancy. However, the reality is that 10–25 percent of women will develop antenatal depression. Unfortunately, most women do not seek treatment.

Whatever the barriers may be, many women continue to suffer throughout their pregnancy. Common barriers include:

- The mother's fear of the effects of treatment on the baby
- Mistaking signs of depression as "normal" pregnancy symptoms
- The social stigma associated with mental illness

In many cases, doctors simply do not recognize the disease in their patients. It is critical for you to speak up because treatment of depression is critical. Suffering from antenatal depression is a risk factor for developing postpartum depression. It carries several other risks as well. Women with depression in pregnancy experience:

- Decreased prenatal care
- Inadequate weight gain because the mother does not meet her own dietary needs
- Increased interventions during delivery
- Increased use of cigarettes, alcohol, and cocaine
- Increased incidence of preterm delivery
- Increased incidence of preecclampsia

Babies suffer as well and show signs of stress if their mothers are untreated. They have high prenatal cortisol and adrenaline (stress hormones) and low dopamine lung tissue and into the chest cavity. He needed chest X-rays and would likely be in the neonatal intensive care unit (NICU) overnight.

My new shift nurse arrived minutes later to my crying and I managed to pull myself together to say, "I need to breastfeed this baby. How am I going to do that here?" She said, "I'll be right back," and returned minutes later with a large electric double breast pump.

If you have ever seen a cow milked in a commercial dairy, you would have some idea of what this operation looked like. I laughed.

---

and serotonin levels (neurotransmitters associated with depression). They also have elevated baseline fetal heart rates.

Babies born to mothers who were depressed during pregnancy suffer decreased APGAR scores, smaller head circumferences, low birth weights, and lower IQs.

The most striking risk to a mother and baby is suicide during pregnancy or postpartum.

Not *If*, but *How*

When we discuss depression during pregnancy, the question is not whether to treat, it's what treatment carries the greatest benefit to mom and baby.

Talk to your physician about what you are experiencing. Mild to moderate cases of antenatal depression respond well to psychotherapy. Your physician may be able to refer you to a therapist who specializes in the treatment of pregnant women. Don't hesitate to inquire about the therapist's training and techniques used. Aside from the technical aspects of connecting with a competent therapist, you must feel comfortable talking to this person. If it is not a good fit, don't hesitate to seek another therapist.

Your doctor may also recommend medication to treat the depression. If you are not sure why he or she is recommending this, don't hesitate to ask. It is often tricky for providers and patients to weigh the risks and benefits of treatment during pregnancy. The evidence on antidepressants during pregnancy is constantly growing, and can be quite confusing. Risks are often broken up into risks in specific trimesters. Organs are formed during the first trimester (the fetal brain, however continues to develop throughout pregnancy). The second and third trimesters are a time of tremendous growth for the fetus. Treatment during these trimesters carries with it concerns about the newborn's adaptation to life outside the womb and respiratory issues. Fortunately, most babies born to mothers who used antidepressants during pregnancy do remarkably well.

Discuss your concerns and your options with your physician today.

Later I showed my mom how I was pumping. "Look, Mom, it's like those things that dairies use!"

I pumped every two hours for fifteen minutes. My nurse was very excited to see bits of colostrum on my second pumping session. I pumped about a quarter of an ounce of colostrum that night and felt very accomplished.

Sander brought videos of our baby from the NICU for me to view. We admired him and agreed to name him Frederick William.

All through the first night I panicked that I would drop Frederick the next day when I held him. I could not get the images out of my mind. I saw him repeatedly falling to the hard linoleum floor. His head would crack. Perhaps he would die or suffer from permanent brain damage. Clearly, I was absolutely irrational. I was lying in bed hooked up to a catheter with bed rails on either side of me. There was no place to drop a baby. But I panicked nonetheless.

My rational side tried to step in: "You can hold a wiggly cat without dropping it. Surely you can hold your baby without dropping him."

But alas, my irrational side won out and I watched reruns of sitcoms all night long to try to shut out the visions in my head.

By morning I began to get antsy that I had not seen Frederick yet. I was told he would be ready that morning but I was not sure how I would get him. I was told that I could visit him as soon as the catheter was out and that it could be removed that morning. I could go in a wheelchair after I produced a requisite amount of urine. Before I pumped I insisted that the catheter be removed. They waited for approval from my midwife. She was on rounds and gave her approval.

I asked for water knowing that I needed it to produce copious amounts of urine. They brought me an 8-ounce plastic cup of water.

"More."

She brought me a small pitcher.

"Do you have a 32-ounce pitcher?"

"Yes."

"Fill up two and bring them to me."

The nurses were amazed at my quick production of urine. I may have set a record.

My midwife arrived to hear the nurses comment on my urine production and I asked about Frederick. She said she would check on when he would be released from the NICU.

We had been separated for about twenty hours at that point. I did not realize at the time that separation of the mother and child can aggravate depression. A difficult birth, a baby with health problems, and just basic disappointment with the failed birth plan all added to my depressive state, as they have with many women before me.

Since I did not know when he would be released or any of the hospital procedures surrounding visiting the NICU and since it is my natural inclination to control the outcome, I decided that I needed to take it on myself to get down to NICU to retrieve him. I could not imagine how I would hold him and move the wheelchair through the halls, so I called home hoping that Sander or my mom could come to the hospital and wheel me to the NICU to get Frederick.

As I was on the phone talking to them at about eight o'clock, a nurse rolled Frederick into my room in one of those Plexiglas bassinets and brought him to my lap. I exclaimed, "He's here, he's here!" and hung up the phone. Frederick opened one eye as he recognized the familiar voice. He had been x-rayed, his lungs had repaired themselves, his breathing was stabilized, and he was released from the NICU.

We were together again. But Frederick was in a C-section drug-induced sleepy state for about ten days postpartum, compounding the problems we would have with his feeding.

3

Feeding Problems

*F*rederick had unusual feeding problems and I was entirely unprepared to deal with them. In my preparation for pregnancy, I read all the natural childbirth books which described the ideal birth: baby is birthed and placed immediately on the mother's belly, amniotic fluid and all. Baby wiggles his way up to the breast and begins to nurse. I did know that my breastfeeding experience might not be quite this idyllic, but at the same time I did not prepare myself by finding all the best breastfeeding resources in the region, *just in case*. I should have.

Considering that a baby only needs food and comfort, there are few stresses as great as when you are unable to feed your baby. An overnight stay in the NICU is never a good omen for breastfeeding. Once Frederick graduated from the NICU, I was visited three times by hospital lactation consultants who tried to help him latch. He sort of latched once but all the attempts were largely unsuccessful. I continued to pump and fed him the breast milk with a cup, a spoon, and an eyedropper.

I began to feel better the day after surgery. I could hobble around and even decided to shower. I got into the shower and my nurse removed my bandages for me. I wailed with pain. I managed to calm myself. I started to shower and was in such pain that I wailed and moaned. I was aware that the people in the adjoining room who shared the shower area were quite concerned. So was Sander. He helped me out of the shower and called the midwife.

"She needs more pain medication. Why is she in so much pain?"

She looked at my chart. "You know Amanda, we're not asking you to be a hero here. You're not taking any pain medication at all."

"I need pain medication."

Pain medication helps a great deal after a C-section, I discovered.

Frederick made it through that second day on the bits of breast milk I was pumping and he had been fed formula the night before in the NICU. By nighttime, he was very hungry and woke often to be fed. We tried and tried. Finally I gave him formula when I was absolutely out of breast milk and he slept a little better. But Sander and I got very little sleep that night.

The nurses were obviously worried about his feeding. My day nurse was very supportive, however, and helped me work with him to latch. Then on Saturday morning, two mornings since the surgery and after a long night with Frederick, I waited for the shift to change and for my nurse to appear again. She was a somewhat nervous and hyper woman but we seemed to understand each other. She ushered my dad and Sander out when I needed to spend two hours trying to get Frederick to latch. She made sure I stayed modestly covered in my hospital gown as I worked to take care of my needs and Frederick's.

That first night with Frederick had been a very long one. And when the shift changed, some other nurse showed up. My nurse did not come. The new nurse was a very rough-around-the-edges woman. Change is a hard thing when you are sleep-deprived and cannot feed your baby. I reported to my midwife that morning that it was time to go home. She said, "I know you have help there, so whenever you feel like you can manage, I will approve it." Between the new nurse and the hourly checks of my vital signs, I was climbing the walls. I had not gotten much sleep. Frederick wasn't feeding. People were driving me crazy.

I put a sign on my hospital door "Do not disturb unless the hospital is on fire or unless you have food." The sign helped.

We prepared to return home. I was told there were no hospital breast pumps available to rent that day. They were all checked out. But I was directed to the manual pump in the hospital kit that would allow me to pump one breast at a time. That was day three of Frederick's life.

On the fifth day of his life, my breasts were engorged and enflamed and Frederick was losing weight. The breastfeeding was not going well. Cup feeding was not effective either. My milk had not yet come in. Sander and my mother took Frederick to the pediatrician first thing Monday morning, on day five.

Our pediatrician insisted that he be supplemented with formula and that we use a bottle.

She said, "He is down to 5 pounds 14 ounces from 6 pounds 7 ounces and he cannot afford to lose any more weight. You can wean him from the bottle later. His mother needs to sleep and eat well. If she is too stressed, there won't be any milk for him. She needs a good breast pump."

Sander was able to acquire an electric breast pump by day six and my engorgement began to improve. Frederick began to get formula regularly in a bottle.

The odd thing, though, about Frederick's bottle feeding sessions is that it took forty-five minutes on average to feed him. One record feeding with a bottle took only twenty minutes, one session took over an hour. Bottle-feeding typically takes about ten minutes. Frederick was also a very tiny baby at just under 6 pounds coming home from the hospital. We were told to feed him every two hours—two hours from the beginning of one feeding to the beginning of the next. We fed him constantly and worked ourselves into exhaustion.

We continued to consult with lactation specialists. About two weeks postpartum, I was still only producing about 60 percent of his needs with my pumping. I was very proud that I had begun producing this much milk because it had taken about ten days for my milk to come in.

But at our visit with the lactation consultant, my pride in my progress was burst when the lactation consultant said, "Sixty percent is good, but your goal should be 100 percent breast milk."

Sander asked on the way home, "Amanda, why are you not able to pump enough milk for Frederick?"

I certainly wondered an awful lot in those days why I was not able to feed my baby. It is supposed to be a natural process and I thought my body would be up to the task. Babies have a God-given right to breastfeed, I was told. And here my baby was with a family of willing caregivers and his mother could not meet his needs for nutrition and he could not even latch.

I did know there was something we could try to increase my milk supply. I responded to Sander, "I am not always able to pump every two hours. If I am taking care of Frederick, I have a hard time finding a fifteen-minute interval to pump."

Sander said, "When it's time to pump, you let me know and I will drop what I am doing. You need to get your milk supply up."

And so I did. With the support of Sander and my mother, I pumped every two hours and gradually built up a suitable milk supply for my son.

In the meantime, Frederick was still not latching. We had eight meetings altogether with the local lactation consultants from the hospital and tried quite a number of tools.

One tool inspired me so much (a supplemental nursing system) that I set a goal for us to be nursing by the following Monday, day twelve. I have always been a goal-driven person and responded to this breastfeeding problem much like I respond to most other problems in my life: make a to-do list, lay out short-term and long-term goals, and move forward. So I had a goal and I communicated it to Frederick and to the other adults of the household.

A Buck a Suck

"OK, Frederick, all you need to do is start with one suck and we will be well on our way to our goal."

The motivational speech did not appeal to Frederick. He still fumbled around rather ineptly. A day passed.

Perhaps Frederick was not sufficiently incentivized.

"Frederick, I'll give you a buck a suck."

No improvement.

"Frederick, I know you are a baby but you need to listen to me and appreciate how many bucks you can make here. Add to those bucks the power of compounding interest and you could well earn yourself a sports car by the time you are in high school."

No improvement.

At some point in this process, we had been red-flagged by the hospital staff because someone called to set up a home visit and we knew that visits were not routine. The lactation consultant nurse who helped us in the hospital showed up to weigh Frederick and to ask about his progress. I was eager to get help latching again, thinking we might have success this time. No luck. I excused myself from the visit twice to cry in the bathroom. As she left she said, "He's just not ready to breastfeed. It's not your fault, you've done all you can do."

A MIRACLE WORKER

That is when I called a good friend of the family. She had called some days before to ask about Frederick's progress. After hearing about our troubles she called her daughter's mother-in-law, who had been a La Leche League leader for years. The mission of La Leche League is to help women breastfeed and this former leader said that she would make it her personal mission to see that Frederick would breastfeed. This news came in the middle of my breastfeeding goal and promising Frederick financial reward to breastfeed. I felt that I had the help I needed from the hospital lactation consultants. I had told her I would get back to her if I needed help. So I got back to her.

My friend then began a search for a renowned lactation consultant in Fresno whom the La Leche League leaders saw as a "miracle worker." As it turned out, most of the family knew this "miracle worker." We had worked with her or her boss in one way or another. This lactation consultant was out of town and we did not see her until about three and a half weeks postpartum.

We drove to Fresno one evening for a five o'clock appointment with her. The lactation consultant arrived and she and Sander exchanged greetings and talked about the small world we live in. I gave her the short version of our story and she said, "OK, let's see how he latches."

I started with a cradle hold and she directed me to use a football hold. She made one adjustment after another: "Move your arm back a little bit this way, bring his head forward just like this, now over a bit, now sit up a bit more."

After a few minutes of her direction, Frederick latched and was nursing. Tears streamed down my face and I worked not to sob.

I said, "He has never latched before."

She replied, "Maybe I am a miracle worker," and started to laugh.

Apparently the label "miracle worker" was her new nickname at her day jobsite, thanks to my friend's phone call to her boss. Her daytime coworkers had no idea of her talents prior to this incident.

"So how does that feel?" she asked.

"It feels like he is biting down on this side as he nurses."

She held his jaw and watched him suckle. "Is that better?"

"Yes."

"I think he may have a jaw problem. I am going to refer you to a chiropractor who works with babies. He's very busy but he will work in babies when he has a cancellation. He doesn't charge for babies either. Can you believe that?"

The appointment with the lactation consultant was Monday evening. On Wednesday, the chiropractor's office called to say he had a cancellation the next day. Also on Wednesday I had decided to nurse Frederick all day—not to use a bottle at all.

It was in that day of nursing that I realized Frederick's nursing behavior was very peculiar. As soon as he latched and sucked, he would pull away and scream. I knew enough about breastfeeding problems at that point that I thought his behavior was due to thrush. I called my lactation consultant and she said, "I thought your nipples looked a bit pink. You poor thing." She instructed me on using an antifungal cream and suggested I call our local pediatrician for a prescription.

We had been using antifungal cream for nearly a day when we arrived at the chiropractor's office. My mom and I took Frederick in for his adjustment and the chiropractor instructed me to place Frederick's bottom in the hole on the exam table. His tiny body was nearly lost in that hole. The chiropractor put his glove-covered pinky into Frederick's tiny mouth and reported to us that Frederick had a swallow reflex on one side of his mouth and a gag reflex on the other. He used gentle adjustment techniques to adjust his jaw.

And then he turned to me and said, "OK."

"OK, what?" I responded.

"Let's see if his latch is better."

I held Frederick to feed him and Frederick looked different. Even that day I could not describe the difference; he looked more settled and peaceful in a very subtle way.

Frederick's latch was much better and he did not want to stop nursing. The chiropractor sent us to Room 6, a room where he does intakes and has no exam tables. Frederick continued to nurse. The chiropractor had told us about a baby he adjusted from the Los Angeles area. The six-month-old baby

Exposed

Our home in Visalia had a master bedroom addition that was the entire second floor of the home. One wall of the bedroom was filled with floor-to-ceiling windows that looked out onto our backyard. When we moved in two years before, we removed the vertical blinds and had not gotten around to replacing them with another window covering. We did not need a window covering for privacy; our lot and those of our neighbors were so filled with trees that we had a great deal of privacy, even perched up on that second story in a neighborhood of single story homes surrounded by fifty-year-old trees.

There was one house directly behind us, however, that had a second story. The house was owned by a couple in their seventies. Their house had a window that looked directly into our backyard and bedroom if they ever opened the curtain.

The curtain remained closed for the two years we lived there. We assumed the room was never used and, therefore, did not worry about privacy issues. We put off purchasing the window coverings.

As I struggled with thrush, I spent quite a number of days in that upstairs bedroom bare chested. Yeast thrives in a dark, moist environment and I figured there was no better way to keep my nipple thrush in check than sitting in a sunny spot in the bedroom, letting the sun filter through those uncovered windows onto my bare breasts.

Some days passed and I continued my thrush therapy.

I woke up one morning and looked across the backyard at the window across the way. The curtain was open for the first time in the two years we had lived there.

We bought some curtains.

had not regained his birth weight. After the adjustment, the baby nursed for twenty-four hours straight.

Frederick wanted to continue nursing as well but I began to feel embarrassed about being there for so long. Frederick had not nursed this much in his entire month-long life.

Truth be told, I finally gave Frederick some milk in a bottle I had ready for him. I didn't want to sit in Room 6 all day long. As we left the office without letting on about the bottle plan, the chiropractor gave me a diet to help with thrush and said that "medication might relieve the symptoms, but the thrush will come back if you don't make these changes."

He suggested a diet low in sugar and grains and high in vegetables, high-quality meats, and beneficial oils.

Frederick was able to nurse but his suck was still very weak and the pain in his mouth from thrush was causing nursing to be more uncomfortable than bottle-feeding. So we decided it would be best to nurse him for the beginning of each feeding and then top him off with a bottle of breast milk. We would wean him off the bottle when the thrush was under control.

Frederick had other plans.

REFUSING THE BOTTLE

When Frederick was five and a half weeks old, ten days or so after his adjustment, Sander woke up to do the early morning feeding, as usual. I woke up to pump but then went back to sleep immediately. I went to a meeting early that morning and my mom took care of Frederick while I was gone. When I returned home I saw a half-empty bottle and asked what was wrong. My mom reported that he had only consumed about an ounce of milk from Sander's early morning feeding and that she had only been able to feed him another ounce.

"But Mom, he would usually have had 11 ounces by now. Do you think he is sick?"

"He seems OK, he just is not interested in eating."

I sat down with Frederick and tried to breastfeed him. He nursed fervently.

"Mom, I don't think he likes those bottles."

After a week of nursing with an adjusted jaw, he refused the bottle and would only have milk straight from the tap. I felt a bit of relief but knew the nursing sessions would be very long with his weak suck. I popped in a movie from our very limited supply and nursed him for more than an hour at a time. His suck improved in about a week. In that week I memorized every scene in *The Sound of Music*. It is ironic that even today Frederick loves the movie, knows the songs and dances, and was greatly disappointed when his preschool teacher, Teacher Maria, did not take him to the mountains for singing and dancing. Preschool was a real disappointment in that regard.

Missing his Infancy

We struggled for weeks with breastfeeding and, in the process, I was told by my midwife and my mother to stop breastfeeding.

My midwife said, "There's more than one way to feed your baby and you don't want to miss his infancy." She was concerned that I was literally driving myself crazy.

My mom said at about four weeks postpartum, "You are missing his infancy and you are jeopardizing your marriage. You need to give up on this."

I could ignore my midwife, but in response to my mother I said, "Mom, now Frederick has thrush and breastfeeding is the only way we are going to get rid of it. Let's work on the thrush and then reassess." I bought myself time.

However, in therapy a year later my therapist was asking me to explore my feelings about the past year. I explained that each time the depression would ease up that a state of grief would overtake me and I did not understand why.

I explained to the therapist all that we went through and our successes in getting Frederick to breastfeed, how content he was as a result, making it through those weeks of screaming, and overcoming all the other obstacles the year brought. I discussed it all as a "win" and it was, so I just did not understand why I was grieving. He asked me a number of times what we lost. I continued to describe what we won. He continued to ask his question until finally I blurted out, *"his infancy."* I started to cry.

In this household we have many times blamed missing Frederick's infancy (particularly the early newborn days) on the breastfeeding problems, but we realize in retrospect that it would have been lost anyway. My depression continued in those early days postpartum even though it was not the most critical element in the household. My mental health was poor but nothing trumps feeding a baby who cannot be fed.

I remember in those early days watching Frederick as he slept. For about two weeks as he slept, his eyes were opened slightly in tiny slits. I became paranoid that demons were spying on me through his eyes. I did know that he was an innocent little guy and going through turmoil of his own, particularly if he was infested with demons. So as he slept beside me in bed, to my left side, I slept on my side and held his tiny right hand in my right hand all night long. I was able to function and care for Frederick, but my own paranoia was palpable. The depression never left.

Nothing Trumps a Baby Who Cannot Be Fed

As difficult as depression is to live with, feeding a baby who cannot be fed brings a whole other level of desperation to an already-taxed household.

I remember when my husband was trying to acquire a hospital-grade breast pump for me to use at home. At first the hospital was out of the pumps but when a pump became available two days later, the lactation consultant explained to my husband that it would cost about $50 a month to rent the pump. She wanted to be sure that he understood the cost and could pay it. There are government programs that will assist low income people with pumps.

I heard Sander say, "I don't care what it costs."

I know that at that moment, as frugal as Sander is, he would have parted with his last dollar and mortgaged anything we had to pay for that pump.

"I just want Frederick to be healthy."

I have never seen Sander so desperate and I have never felt so desperate myself. We cannot know how much more severe my depression became because of those very desperate six weeks, but it most certainly had an impact.

For my part, I will be forever grateful to the ladies of La Leche League in Fresno and their miracle worker lactation consultant who have committed many decades to helping babies like Frederick become healthy children. And as it turns out, researchers find that breastfeeding reduces stress in new moms (Mezzacappa and Katlin 2002). As more women are able to get such good-quality help sooner with such a basic need, postpartum stress may decrease, and so too may the rates and severity of postpartum depression.

4

Back with a Vengeance

The late summer and early fall of 2002 provided a nice break for our family in the larger scheme of things. Frederick was feeding well, we began to catch up on our sleep, and we were settling into life with an infant. My mom and I took several trips together in a short two-month period. We attended an event in Berkeley to help break the Guinness Book of World Records record for the number of women breastfeeding simultaneously. I was one of more than 1,130 women who set a new record that was only recently broken by a group of women and babies in Manila. We visited Santa Barbara and had the rare opportunity to room in one of the Mission dormitories that the Franciscans have since sold. We later traveled to the Central Coast of California again to give Frederick his first experience putting his toes into the ocean. I was still very tired, but we were getting by. I thought I was getting better.

In late October of 2002, at six months postpartum, life was no longer improving. Suddenly I found myself with no patience for anyone nor for any task. I found myself crying regularly for little reason. It was difficult for me to care for Frederick in those times.

My mother, who had been living with us about half the time, moved in full-time at this point. There was one memorable time when she was headed off to house-sit for someone for a week, about an hour away.

As she left she said to Sander, "If you need me to come back for any reason, you call me." She packed her car and left.

Sander found me sobbing in the room and called my mom before she reached her destination. My mom visited a friend for a couple hours and returned back to our house to live for more than a year. She then purchased the house across the street so that she could be closer. In all those months there were several times that she took Frederick away from me when she found me sobbing uncontrollably and trying to care for him.

Obsessive-Compulsive Behavior

My slight tendency toward obsessive-compulsive behavior worsened. I remember vividly being in a therapy session describing my obsessive-compulsive symptoms.

The therapist said, "Give me an example of what kinds of things bother you."

"Well, let's say that I don't want that book on the couch because I think it really belongs on the table. I am unable to move it because I am sitting with Frederick nursing him. I try to get the book out of my mind. My rational voice tries to tell me it doesn't matter that the book is on the couch. I stare at the book and the book begins to make me very anxious."

"If you get to the point of asking someone to move the book, how would the conversation go?" he asked.

"I would exclaim 'get the damned book off the couch!'"

As my exclamation came out of my mouth in the therapist's office, it sounded very funny to my ears, so I clarified, "But it wouldn't sound that funny, it would be much grumpier."

But just as I was clarifying the tone I would use to get someone to move the book off the couch, I realized what I was seeing in his face. He didn't think my first version was funny at all.

Before becoming depressed I was a very rule-oriented person. I would make household rules that would help govern how things *should be* in the house. Kitchen knives should not be washed in the dishwasher because it reduces their sharpness. The dishwasher had to be organized according to my rules to make sure everything got washed effectively. A particular sponge should be used to wash the dishes. Hot tap water was not to be used for cooking.

Rules can be a good thing. They help you determine what is important, how things *should* be. But my rules have always bordered on being a bit compulsive. In my depression, I added rules and I became more obsessed. My family worked hard to live with me.

ANXIETY

Once again, I became frustrated easily by people and situations. As during the pregnancy, Sander began to check my e-mail and answer the phone to limit my anxiety over people contact. I began therapy and as a result of some of those sessions, I began to draw boundaries with some of the people in my work. When those boundaries were not observed, I quit the contracts. These small moves were setting some of the structures in place that helped me survive in those months.

I insisted that the front door of the house stay closed so that people could not see in through the screen door. My rationale was that if someone came to the door and I did not want to speak to them, I did not want to feel obligated to do so. If the door was opened, I would obsess on the door all day and worry about who might show up. One day I was sitting in our bedroom at the top of the stairs when my mom came over. She left the front door open and came upstairs. From the rocker upstairs, you could look down and see the door. I noticed it was open. "The door's open Mom, I don't want anyone to see me up here!" She shut the door.

In addition to keeping that door closed, we took our walks in off hours. My mom and I took Frederick out to a neighboring community college and to the downtown area. In both cases, we went in the evening when the students were gone and when the stores were closed. We typically walked at dusk. There would still be a few people and we felt safe enough, but not overwhelmed by people. One night we tried walking on the track at the community college with all the other walkers. The regulars were friendly and conversant. I felt anxious and claustrophobic. We never went on the track again.

Therapists call my strategies "avoidance," so even in trying to cope in my poor mental state, I was revealing my illness. Avoidance of people and circumstances and isolating myself in my home were not signs of a healthy person.

OBSESSION WITH DEATH

I did not have thoughts of suicide in these days, but I did become rather obsessed with my own death and upset by my thoughts. Quite often in my down cycles I wondered if I would be killed as I drove downtown or walked across the street. My own reaction to my thoughts varied from "good, let's get it over with" to vivid images of how my death might come.

In all my days, depressed and not, my rational side always tries to respond to my irrational thoughts. If the thoughts are unlikely, my rational side can talk my irrational side out of the thoughts. In these dark days, my "rational" side became increasingly irrational. Its primary job, after all, was to convince me that my irrational side was, in fact, irrational. And so its analysis of my death obsessions went something like this:

> *"Death is not very likely and if it comes, that's not really the worst case for the family, so you shouldn't worry too much about that. What you should worry about is if you are critically wounded and can't care for yourself or Frederick, then Sander and Mom will have to care for you both. But unless your breasts are amputated or burned, Frederick will still be able to breastfeed even if you are in a coma."*

My obsessive-compulsive side ran related visions in my head of losing my breasts or of hospital staff rolling my comatose body to the other side and moving Frederick so that he could nurse on the other breast. I wondered how he would feel about me when I was in a coma. Would he understand that I still loved him even if I could not speak to him, look at him, or hold him?

Clearly, my "rational" side did not always do me any favors.

In this period, a good friend of the family who is a licensed clinical social worker asked me how I was feeling. She asked me generally, "What is your worst fear with this depression?" I explained that I was worried that I would end up in an institution and Frederick would be taken away from me. She began to talk with me about medication.

MEDICATION

Our friend was of the few trained people in the field who saw how serious my depression was. With other doctors, I put on a good face, not to try to hide anything from them intentionally, that was just my public face. This is how I operated in any relationship outside of family, to the degree it was possible. My chiropractor asked me in the fall of 2002 if I had contemplated suicide and I told her my visions about being comatose and the hospital staff rolling me over and helping Frederick latch. My chiropractor laughed. I am sure that I told the story in an amusing way. That is what I did in public. But our friend heard enough reports from my mom and saw me enough to know that my case was serious.

We visited her house one day and she took me aside to explain why I needed to take medication. She described to me that my brain chemistry was out of balance and that medication would be the only way to bring it into balance again. Even when my hormones were back in balance, my brain chemistry would have been so fouled up by the episode that it would never be straight again except with medication. She argued that I had no choice but to take medication; that it might take time to find the right medication for me, and that once I found the right medication, I should expect to be on it for six months. She stressed the need for medication if we planned to have another baby. With another pregnancy, we would know what medication worked for me and would be able to use it if necessary.

I felt devastated hearing this advice because I had avoided medication for so long. I did not know what the impact would be on Frederick. The relatively short history of antidepressant use and my own obsessive-compulsive tendencies were difficult to reconcile. But on my good days I did some research and began to strategize about how to reduce Frederick's exposure to medication.

I read research on the half-life of Zoloft done by Pfizer and found that the half-life was twenty-six hours and that the peak concentration of the medication in the bloodstream occurs between 4.5 and 8.4 hours after taking the dose. I knew that the content of medication in my breast milk would relate to the content in my bloodstream at the time that Frederick was nursing. My plan was to night wean Frederick and take the medication as soon as he went to sleep. If he would sleep for eight to ten hours, he would likely miss the peak concentration of Zoloft in my bloodstream.

Two problems stood in the way of my plan. First, Frederick did not sleep through the night consistently until he was nearly four years old. Second, I was afraid of taking the medication. I remembered the narcotic drug I received with my surgery for pain relief. In those early days postpartum, I took that narcotic, lay in bed and hallucinated. It was a pretty cool feeling, actually, and the day I realized I wanted to keep taking the narcotic is also the day I quit. We have a lot of addiction problems in our family, I display a great deal of addictive behavior myself, and I had read a lot about problems people have weaning themselves from depression medication. I did not need another problem.

And truth be told, I obsessed about the effect of the medication on me. Whether it would have been rational at the time to take Zoloft was irrelevant. *I could not make a rational decision.* I held off and searched for other options.

5

Searching for
Answers While Depressed

*A*s my friend pressed the need for medication, we hit the six month mark postpartum and my mood took a severe turn. We knew immediately what was coming and we began to respond. I made an appointment with our family practice doctor and I spoke with another doctor in our team of professionals.

Both doctors steered me away from depression medication. The family practice doctor's words were what shaped my path in a general sense. What he said to me made me mad at first. He can have a rough bedside manner. Actually, his abrasive tendencies are part of his charm when you are feeling well.

To me in my depressed state, his suggestion sounded something like, "All women have hormonal changes in pregnancy, but not all get depressed. What's your problem?" Anger welled up within me and I headed home. I reflected on his words and searched the far reaches of my rational brain. I realized what he intended for me to hear and it appealed to me:

> "Amanda, all women have hormonal changes as a result of pregnancy,
> but not all end up with postpartum depression. You need to find out
> why you have depression. Why has this hit you when it does not hit
> all women? Medication will only cover up the symptoms and will never
> allow you to find the answers."

He happened to appeal to my analytical core in making his statement and I began to wonder, "Why is it that I am depressed?" What are the explanatory factors that cause depression symptoms in one group and not in the other? It became a mission of mine to find out the underlying cause of my own depression. Looking back, my "mission" was rather amusing not because it was unimportant, but because I was in no condition whatsoever for a mission of any kind.

I muddled my way through my search, madly obsessing over one potential cause and then another. I had few tools of my own to examine why I might be different. As a depressed person, I was not my very best advocate. So I floated from one possible cause to another for a year and a half, improving my condition a bit each time before I finally received some relief from a treatment plan.

Corn Allergies

In my search for answers I began to see a chiropractor regularly. A friend told me that chiropractic adjustments would help my body function better and I would get some relief from depression as a result. My depressed and increasingly surly side was not all too convinced, but part of me thought it was worth a try. I began to get regular adjustments. It was in this office that I found my greatest relief, but it took well over one year.

My chiropractor suggested that corn in my diet was contributing to my depression. Symptoms include depression, disturbed sleep, fatigue, headache, joint pain, and many others.

My rational side began to become very skeptical and, of course, my irrational side became irate. Surely something as benign as corn was not the cause of this madness. At this point my mom started seeing my chiropractor as well and she, too, had corn allergies. My mom said that we would try the one-month no-corn diet that the chiropractor recommended. I would have never done the diet without her prodding. It simply made no sense to me at the time.

But because of my mother's leadership, we followed the no-corn diet. We discovered that corn was in nearly all processed foods and so for one month, we made all our own dressings and sauces and cooked from scratch.

It was a difficult month for eating. I dreamed all month of my corn feast day. My chiropractor had explained that we were to give up corn entirely for one month and then we would have one day when we feasted on it. She explained that if we were allergic to corn, this test would tell us.

My corn feast dream included two bowls of corn flakes for breakfast, lunch at a Mexican restaurant starting with corn chips and ending with at least two tamales, and dinner at another Mexican restaurant with more corn chips and enchiladas. Perhaps I would have additional bowls of corn flakes as snacks throughout the day. And surely somewhere I could find some of those "corn nuts" that I hadn't seen in years. I deserved them.

Corn feast day came some time in early January of 2003. I ate my corn flakes and excitedly headed to a Mexican restaurant downtown for an early lunch. I ate a whole basket of corn chips by myself and sat editing a report while waiting for the enchiladas. This restaurant did not have tamales, so I was a bit disappointed. I ordered the crab enchiladas—they are made with the imitation crab that includes corn starch. I was in corn heaven.

By the time I was finishing my enchiladas, my vision began to get blurry. I had a difficult time reading my report. My head became fuzzy and I lost my focus. I finished my enchiladas and made a beeline home. As I drove home I hoped that I would make it. My vision got more blurry and my head began to pound. I arrived home and headed straight to bed as I announced to the household, "I feel like shit with legs!"

It appeared I had a corn allergy. It was hard for my rational or irrational side to refute this very clear evidence, although I still had depression. What I discovered was that corn allergies are actually very common and the symptoms include depression and fuzzy thinking.

Apparently corn allergies can be due to overexposure of corn. Corn is in everything these days. It is used in foods as fillers, its oil is used to fry foods, and it is the most common sweetener in soft drinks and other sweet processed foods. Some years after my corn feast day and years of avoiding corn, I can eat corn now and then. I keep planning to eat popcorn again, someday.

The corn episode helped me stick with the chiropractor a little longer, even though I was depressed, cynical, and felt as if I would never be better again.

Counseling

I entered therapy in February of 2003 as I took another downturn in my depression. For a six-week period I was seeing a therapist and a chiropractor once a week and quite rapidly spending our savings. To make matters worse in the finance department, the therapist helped me see that a relationship with one of my clients was not working well. I did not expect this to be an issue in therapy at all, but I arrived one day frustrated that I could not get the information I needed from the client's staff to meet a deadline. As he probed me, I described a long history of such a relationship.

Leave it to a therapist to help you draw boundaries, which may or may not be accepted by the other party. Those contracts made up most of my work that year. The cost of my therapy was an hour's drive to Fresno once a week, $110 an hour in fees, and a whole lot of money in contracts.

The therapy did help me with my struggle and drawing boundaries is a really good idea. But I ran out of time and money and did not continue my one-hour trek to the therapist. If I had to do it again, I would have started therapy in pregnancy and continued it for about two years postpartum. In the middle of the madness, it is difficult to judge what therapies are critical to the cause.

Yeast Overgrowth

Frederick and I both had thrush in his infancy. Thrush is simply a surface-based fungal infection. It is the same fungus that is treated in women with vaginal yeast infections, which is caused by an overgrowth of the fungus *Candida albicans*. Babies can have an overgrowth in their mouths, which causes painful sores. The sores are often white, but not necessarily so. Moms can have an overgrowth on their nipples which causes nipple pain during nursing. Thrush is extremely painful, but it is just an overgrowth on your surface areas and, at the end of the day, can be treated fairly easily if caught early.

One of my doctors counseled me that *candida* could spread to other areas of the body, including organs. As you might imagine, *candida* became one of the objects of my obsession. I was told that it is fed by sugar.

One evening I went shopping and passed the bakery area. I could not stop thinking about the chocolate-covered donuts. Donuts had not appealed to me in years. After obsessing for some time and trying to talk myself out of it, I bought the donut and ate it in the parking lot. The signs of thrush reappeared the next day.

I came to realize that as the thrush cycled up and down, I would crave sugar in some insane fashion just before an outbreak.

The sugar-outbreak cycle fed my obsession with both candida and sugar.

The thrush came and went for nearly a year and at some point I just accepted it and no longer obsessed over it. In the early days I boiled everything in the house and cleaned obsessively when an outbreak occurred. The outbreaks continued and so my diligence declined. But I did continue to read about it.

In late March of 2003 when I felt shooting pains in my breasts while nursing, I had read so much about thrush that I knew immediately I had a serious case. I called my chiropractor to say, "I have shooting pains in my breasts while I am breastfeeding and I know it is from yeast in my milk ducts. What do I do?" She researched the problem and called me back.

She said, "I have a program you can follow, but you cannot do it while you are breastfeeding. You might consider weaning Frederick at eighteen months and following this program. Research shows that the most benefits from breast milk come in the first eighteen months."

"I will not wean Frederick. It took too much to get him to breastfeed and he will wean when he wants. What else do you have for me?"

"Amanda, I'm not going to kid you. This diet is going to suck. But this is what you have to do for three months: eliminate sugar and anything that breaks down as sugar. That includes grains, fruit, and lactose. Eliminate all high mold foods including mushrooms, cheese, peanuts, and cashews. Eliminate all fermented foods. Eliminate beans."

"What do I eat?" I asked sheepishly.

"Vegetables and meat," she responded.

"How about the smallest red potatoes from our garden?" I asked, since they were lower in carbohydrates.

"No."

"What about the smallest sprinkling of the lowest carbohydrate bean in a salad?"

"No."

I hung up the phone and followed the diet for over six months.

The only reason I was able to be so diligent is that I had company. The morning I started the diet I visited my mom and gave her the bad news. I was headed to a business meeting and she was staying with a friend in the same town for a few days. I stopped to visit. She proceeded to report to me about her bad day.

In response to her comments I said, "Oh, so you think you've had a bad day, guess what diet I started on this morning?" I explained what my chiropractor told me and pointed to the almonds I was carrying—the only thing I had eaten since the phone call (since it was the only portable food I had that fit the diet).

She said, "OK. I will do the diet with you."

Candida and Other "Gut" Problems

If your intestinal tract is not up to speed, you will not fully digest all of the nutrients in your diet. Nutrients are critical in the depression fight, as you will see in the second half of this book. If you have the typical signs and symptoms, consider the lab work that I list in the Appendix. For further reading see Elizabeth Lipski's *Digestive Wellness*.

Signs of intestinal dysbiosis	Associated conditions
gas and bloating	eczema
abdominal pain	celiac disease
food sensitivities	Crohn's disease
constipation	allergies
diarrhea	

And so she did.

The candida diet was incredibly difficult. We still reflect on those long, hard days in the spring of 2003. We could not eat anything we considered to be food and we were extremely crabby.

About one month into the *candida* diet, in April of 2003, I noticed that my updated driver's license had not arrived from the Department of Motor Vehicles, even though I had taken the test and a new photo in February. I called to inquire and they asked me to come in for a new picture. I felt terrible, still in the middle of yeast die-off, but I managed to drag myself to the office anyway. I remember standing in front of the camera, mustering up my best smile, and acting as if I felt fine.

About two weeks later I received my new license in the mail and I cried. I looked great in the picture. You would think that for as bad as I felt on the day I took the picture, I would have looked terrible. And I looked far better than I looked in 1998, when I took my previous picture for a California driver's license. Back in 1998 we had just moved from Michigan and I was at the peak of my health quest. I had been shedding my graduate student pounds and eating limited animal products.

I showed the pictures to my chiropractor and she said, "No offense Amanda, but in this earlier picture you look like your older sister." The "older" picture was taken five years before; in both pictures I weighed 170 pounds, though I looked much heavier in the earlier picture. I cried when I received the license because I knew that pasta and bread would be distant memories in my life. I despised the candida diet, but this picture vindicated it.

After two months of hell on the candida diet, we began to feel better. As we felt better and reflected on my driver's license picture, we realized that we could never again return to the old diet.

The diet change did appear to help my digestion and it guaranteed that my diet would be more nutrient dense. We ate about 5 pounds of produce a day in the household, good quality meats, and absolutely no packaged foods. We should continue to eat that way, but ironically, as I have become less obsessed with everything, I find it increasingly difficult to cut out any crumb that may come from a grain product or every sweet piece of fruit I can smell in our home orchard. I do try to reduce grains and I indulge in fruit while gardening. Gardeners deserve that sort of decadence (and we all deserve the vitamin C, folate, and antioxidants in the fruit).

The *candida* fight did help my depression as well because of the whole-foods diet rich in produce, but it did not take care of the problem completely. My down cycles came less frequently, but they were still severe when they hit. I continued to visit the chiropractor, hoping for more help.

Heavy Metal Toxicities

In the middle of our candida die-off in the spring of 2003, my chiropractor called with a suggestion that I get tested for heavy metal toxicity. She explained that toxic levels of some heavy metals could lead to depression. The cost was one ten-day period using Johnson & Johnson's Baby Shampoo, 50 dollars, and some lost strands of hair. I was game. I used the shampoo religiously for two weeks (though for the record, you can really use any shampoo; I was just being compulsive in using a shampoo that the laboratory preferred). By the time my hair was sufficiently greasy and nasty (because baby shampoo does not do all that I was used to), I was ready for the test. My mom cut strands of hair from various places on the back of my head and put the root ends in the test envelope. We mailed the kit out in the regular mail.

About two weeks later the results came back with a shocking discovery: I had extremely high levels of uranium in my body. I was at the ninety-eighth percentile among the laboratory's population. On the lab report it listed "depression" as a possible outcome of uranium toxicity. But my rational side said there was no way I could have been exposed to that much uranium. There must be a clinical error. We conducted a test at another national laboratory. Two more weeks and a greasy head of hair later, we sent off the second hair sample. The second set of results confirmed the first. I had high levels of uranium in my body.

I began to panic about uranium being in my breast milk. I wondered how I would detoxify my body without flooding my breast milk with uranium.

My chiropractor spoke with some colleagues about my case and she heard a number of things that caused me to panic even more:

- Uranium has no known chelating agent, a chemical used in complementary medicine that binds to the offending metals and helps it exit the body. Uranium lodges tightly into your bones and stays there.
- Frederick was already exposed to uranium in utero and likely had high levels as well.

The Environmental Protection Agency (EPA) in its fact sheet on uranium says:

About 99 percent of the uranium ingested in food or water will leave a person's body in the feces, and the remainder will enter the blood. Most of this absorbed uranium will be removed by the kidneys and excreted in the urine within a few days. A small amount of the uranium in the bloodstream will deposit in a person's bones, **where it will remain for years**. (Bold added.)

I was in full panic mode. I had found the cause of my depression, had no way to fix it, and my child had the same condition. I began to worry about Frederick's future struggle with depression and our future fight with bone cancer. The EPA mentions the risks to health of uranium toxicity in its same fact sheet:

The greatest health risk from large intakes of uranium is toxic damage to the kidneys, because, in addition to being weakly radioactive, uranium is a toxic metal. Uranium exposure also increases your risk of getting cancer due to its radioactivity. Since uranium tends to concentrate in specific locations in the body, risk of cancer of the bone, liver cancer, and blood diseases (such as leukemia) are increased.

I began to theorize about how I was exposed. It may have happened on one of my trips to Eastern Europe in the 1990s. When Sander and I visited Poland in 1994 we heard stories about nuclear by-products being widely available. Perhaps Sander and I were both exposed unknowingly. Or perhaps I had been exposed alone on my trip in the summer of 1990. But then again, there was always the possibility that it was my mother who had been exposed as a result of fallout from Hiroshima during her time on Okinawa after World War II, in her young days as an Air Force brat. The possibilities were endless for a person obsessed with the world around her.

I wanted to confirm how I was exposed to make sure that I was no longer being exposed. So we all had tests. Sander and my mom ended up with greasy hair as well because I insisted that they use Johnson & Johnson baby shampoo. We sent their hair test kits in a few weeks later. If Sander and I were high in uranium, that finding would lend credence to the Poland theory. If my mom and I were high, that finding would lend credence to the Okinawa theory. Of course, if my mom and I were high that might also necessitate testing my sister and my uncle, my mom's brother who also lived on Okinawa.

I had plans to test quite a number of permutations of family members. I spent many hours speculating on where the uranium came from and who, as a result, would be contaminated and needed to be tested. A test result as unusual as uranium toxicity on top of a postpartum mood disorder was a bad combination. I spent the better part of the summer of 2003 looking under every rock for uranium.

My own paranoia over the uranium stood in sharp contrast to the calm of one of our doctors. He insisted that the uranium came from our drinking water and said, "We've all got high levels here." I said, "But we have a water distiller. It distills metals." He chuckled at my naiveté. "Nothing distills uranium."

Both my mom and Sander's results came back with very high levels of uranium. My mom's levels were higher than mine; she was in the ninety-ninth percentile. Sander was in the seventy-fifth percentile. Our levels fit our doctor's claim about the water. I found public documents about well water tests in our area and found that there was a good bit of uranium in the water.

Though the levels did not reach the maximum contaminant level as defined by the Environmental Protection Agency, the uranium was still present. One report of a nearby well showed levels roughly one-half the maximum contamination level as defined by the EPA.

One doctor suggested a program to flush the uranium out of my body. He recommended 1200 mg of MCHC calcium a day (a highly digestible bovine-based calcium) and a no-grain diet focused on vegetables, lamb or beef, olive oil, and cod liver oil. Uranium competes with calcium for residence in bone cells. As bones regenerate, uranium may be dislodged and the new slots would be filled with calcium (if all goes well). The highly absorbable MCHC calcium would help increase the likelihood that the new cells would be filled with calcium.

I was on the candida diet at the time anyway, which was basically the diet the doctor recommended to me. I added the MCHC calcium and my uranium levels declined 40 percent in six months, while I continued to live in the same location with uranium in our water. I had gotten rid of corn, candida, and a lot of uranium but the depression continued and I kept searching.

AMINO ACIDS

In the fall of 2003 my chiropractor attended a conference at which a presenter discussed one of his cases. His patient had severe depression and did not want to be medicated. She had an amino acids profile done, which determined that she was low in amino acids. She was supplemented and her depression improved. My chiropractor sent me home with an amino acid bloodspot test kit.

I was at one of my low points when I returned home with the test, yet eager to get results. I fasted overnight and tried to administer the bloodspot test to myself using the lancets that were provided in the test kit. The first lancet broke and provided no blood. The second one worked and provided one small drop of blood that in no way covered the two circles required for the test.

I remembered my high school biology days when we were given the assignment to check our blood types in class. Lab partners were supposed to prick other students' fingers with a lancet and help squeeze blood onto the blood type test paper. One boy in the class could not get his finger to stop bleeding. My partner Martha kept saying, "Mandy, I'm so sorry," as she pricked and re-pricked my finger trying to get enough blood out for the test. I knew that day in high school that I was the lucky one with blood that clotted so easily. However, on this day, trying to provide enough blood for my amino acids test, I was becoming increasingly obsessed at getting the blood out and also extremely frustrated knowing that I probably would not be successful, given my lesson in high school biology.

I searched the house looking for objects to pierce my finger. I sterilized two needles and tried to puncture my finger. I considered the Henckels knives in the kitchen. After considering the knives, I got a bit more rational and called all my medical providers for extra lancets. No one could provide help. All the while, I was starving and so finally ate in the middle of the morning. My fast was broken and I had no tools to complete the test.

The company sent another test kit, but I was so upset by the first episode that I knew I could not take the test alone. I might literally kill myself. I asked a neighbor who had spent years as a nurse, including time in World War II, to procure a number of extra lancets and to administer the test. It took a few weeks for her to remember to pick up the lancets and another week or two for me to remember to fast and walk to her house. I discovered that with the proper training and tools, it really is not a big deal to supply the blood for a small bloodspot test.

I mailed the test kit just before Christmas and the results were ready by the New Year; however, it was February 13, 2004, before I would actually begin to benefit from the results. With my own effort to block out the lancet fiasco and with some communication errors, it was early February before we were reviewing the results. By then I was in the middle of a major depressive slump and had difficulty even attending a doctor's appointment without a breakdown. I made an appointment to see the chiropractor and she called the clinician at the lab to discuss my results.

According to the clinician, my amino acids profile was "one of the worst he has ever seen" (though they have seen much worse since). The test measured all eight essential amino acids and three additional amino acids. I was low in seven amino acids, borderline in one, and had normal levels in two. He said that my profile suggested I was also extremely low in B vitamins.

I knew that B vitamin deficiencies aid in the development of candida overgrowth, so my rational side decided that these test results might be valid. But regardless, I decided that there was an easy way to know if amino acids would help my depression: the company offered a customized amino acid supplement. My chiropractor asked the clinician if he expected me to see an improvement in my depression with the supplement. He said, "As bad as those results are, I expect a dramatic improvement." There was nothing to lose but some start-up dollars.

My depression had reached a low point again and I suddenly had hope that I would find relief. The supplement would arrive in one week, on Friday, February 13, 2004, and my life would change. We went to see *The Vagina Monologues* on Friday the 13th with a friend and I said, "I just started taking this supplement today and it's going to be a whole new world soon."

He responded, "Amanda, please, if it doesn't work, don't do anything rash," as only one sufferer from depression could say to another.

On Friday, I took about one quarter of the dosage of amino acids, two times a day. The directions suggested that starting with a full dose could lead to stomach upset. I handled the one-quarter dose well. I increased my intake to a one-half dose by Sunday and a full dose by Tuesday. By Tuesday I began to feel some relief from my depression. By Thursday I was a new person.

Around day seven I remember sitting in the bedroom together with my mom and Sander in the evening after Frederick went to sleep. I was so excited about how I was feeling I told my mom and Sander how sad it was that they, too, were not taking amino acids. I went from a major depressive slump to feeling great within a week. And I continued to feel good.

By early March we put our house on the market. I was feeling so good that I decided to list the house "for sale by owner." We acted for about a month as our own agents, but I had just volunteered to write a million-dollar grant application, so I decided not to push my energy and we enlisted a realtor. I spent my time writing the grant application, which did not get funded but, more importantly, did not drive me crazy.

By Memorial Day we had moved out of our house entirely and I was tired, but I was not depressed. The slump in February vanished suddenly with the amino acids supplementation and the depression had not returned even in the midst of a major life change.

Two Steps Forward, One Step Back

Life continued to be good and manageable for another year. I continued on a less strict *candida*-like diet, low in carbohydrates and high in whole foods and nutrients. But over many months I began to gain weight slowly. My mental health was good but I would arrive at my doctor's appointments and say, "I feel fine, but why am I getting so fat?" My energy slowly faded as well over all those months until I found myself unable to work once again, but this time because of exhaustion. Finally one day one of my doctors looked at me with a keen eye and said, "You have a thyroid problem."

A new amino acid panel showed that I was still low in amino acids and the amino acid panel suggested other nutritional deficiencies as well. I remember my chiropractor giving me the results and saying, "You are still low in folic acid."

"But I can't be low in folic acid, I have a good diet."

My diet had improved but sometimes diets do not change fast enough or drastically enough to take care of past sins. My digestion had improved as well but again, not as quickly and as drastically as was necessary.

I went home with my proverbial tail between my legs and started thinking about my ongoing health crises since giving birth. I began to read. For the first time, I began to read about depression. Depressed people do not tend to read and depression survivors are too busy catching up with life to read about depression. But my mental state was good and this newfound health problem inspired a reading frenzy. What I was struck by was how low folic acid can be related to both depression and hypothyroidism.

The ladies of this house began to talk about this issue. The ladies, of course, are my mom and I, both with our own postpartum depression war wounds. My mom's mom would have something to say as well if she did not die twenty-five years ago in her early sixties and we even speculate that her own mother (my great-grandmother) would be able to comment if she had not died at about the age of fifty of heart failure.

All of us had health problems that extended from the postpartum period onward, four generations of women on the maternal side of my family. But my mother was a different case among the ladies of the family because she did, in fact, get ahold of her health problems. She is a youthful looking sixty-year-old, in stark contrast to the two generations before her who were not only not youthful, but never even made it to retirement age. I quizzed my mom about those years back in the 1970s.

"When did you notice a change in your postpartum depression?" I asked.

"About a year after you were born, I developed a severe case of arthritis and was immobilized by it. About the same time, *Prevention Magazine*, which was in its infancy, ran an article on alleviating arthritis through diet. I followed the diet diligently and the arthritis went away. The funny thing was that the postpartum depression went away too."

"What was the diet?"

She thought for a moment and said, "A whole-foods, high protein and vegetable diet, much like what we are doing now."

We stared at each other in silence.

She continued on that diet for many years and she kept both the arthritis and depression at bay. Her depression returned when her diet declined.

I expect that whatever nutrient imbalance caused my mom's postpartum depression also proceeded unchecked and caused the arthritis. The arthritis diet fixed the problem that caused both ailments and she was able to move out of the postpartum period in good health. My grandmother and perhaps her mother as well were not quite as lucky. The nutrient imbalances that immobilized them postpartum wreaked havoc on their bodies and led them to early death.

This book is dedicated to these ladies who died decades too soon because the medical knowledge of the day did not even recognize the condition called postpartum depression, much less help them resolve the health problems that followed. Remembering them and feeling a sense of loss in their brief years provided me with motivation to research this issue and to incorporate the research into this book.

There are answers. There are tools.

In the following chapters, I describe the research I found and highlight the nutrient deficiencies most commonly associated with depression in the medical literature. Those deficiencies can cause a host of other problems and are best fixed now to increase your chances of a long life in good health.

Deficits in a World of Plenty

*B*efore we delve too much deeper into the answers, into nutrients and their association with depression, we should spend a few pages talking about how common nutrient deficiencies are. Many people will tell you that nutrient deficiencies are very rare in the United States and in other advanced industrial countries. We have access to fresh food, all year long. Why would we ever end up deficient in nutrients?

Look on the list of ingredients of your nutritious breakfast cereal or the snack food you pick up from a quick stop. What ingredients do you see? When thiamin is listed as an ingredient, it was added in the manufacturing process. It is not native to the cereal grain. Folic acid, thiamin, riboflavin, magnesium, zinc, and other nutrients are commonly added to cereals.

Have you ever wondered why companies add vitamins and minerals to your food?

First, it is marketing. A nutritional label with 45 percent of your daily value of zinc might get your attention. As consumers are becoming more nutrition oriented, we might choose the food item with added nutrients over one that adds as little as possible. Moms looking for healthy snacks for their children might compare the iron or calcium content of two products and choose the one with more nutrients. We may be likely to choose the "fortified" foods as a result because of their impressive lists of nutrients. Fortified foods have become popular because we are more nutrient conscious.

Second, our food is fortified because there would be severe nutritional consequences otherwise. The folic acid campaign in the United States is the key example. In the 1990s, the Food and Drug Administration in the United States required that grain products be fortified with folic acid. Our foods are fortified with folic acid because without the added vitamin, most of us would be dangerously low in this key nutrient. Low intake of folic acid or food folate in pregnant women is associated with neural tube defects (such as spina bifida) in our babies.

Look at the label on your cereal box and note the level of folic acid. It is in your cereal because the food processing company is required to add it, not because Mother Nature put it there. If folic acid did not get added to our grains, not only would we have more incidences of neural tube defects in this country, we might have higher rates of depression as well. You will see that in the next chapter. So in this sense, fortification of our food may be a good thing, though it is not without potential pitfalls and remains controversial among nutritionists.

The fact that we live in a world in which a boxed cereal can supply adequate folic acid is evidence to some that, with such impressive technology, we are not likely to be nutrient deficient. The government will continue to respond to widespread nutrient deficiencies with government policy as it has with folic acid.

But as far as I am concerned, if you are still deficient today in folic acid or in magnesium and it is aggravating your depression, you probably do not want to wait around for government action. I certainly do not recommend it.

So how likely is it that your nutritional intake is inadequate today?

You will probably be surprised. Let's look at the data.

The U.S. Department of Health and Human Services conducts an ongoing food survey called the National Health and Nutritional Examination Survey (NHANES). Thousands of people are interviewed about their food intake. If they report that they eat one cup of broccoli and three scallops a day, the NHANES team determines the nutrient profile of that food intake from a massive food database collected and maintained by the United States Department of Agriculture (USDA). For every survey respondent, the NHANES team determines their nutrient intake. With the survey sampling techniques, we get a pretty fair idea of what people in the United States eat.

Based on the 2001–02 survey, we should be thankful that folic acid is added to our food. Note table 6.1 below. I present the average intake of various nutrients as determined by the 2001–02 NHANES survey in the first column. I also provide the twenty-fifth percentile value—25 percent of respondents fall at or under that nutrient intake. The dietary reference intake (DRI) is in the third column and my commentary is in the fourth.

First, take a look first at magnesium. The DRI is 320 milligrams. The average intake for women nineteen and older is 240 milligrams. Twenty-five percent of us do not even consume 200 milligrams of magnesium a day. How bad is our intake of magnesium? Very bad. Most of us are likely deficient. And this has implications for depression.

What about iron? We should be eating at least 18 milligrams of iron a day. On average, we eat 13 milligrams and the bottom quarter of us eat about 10 milligrams a day—nearly half the amount we should be consuming according to the government. I also consider that intake to be "very bad."

As a country, our zinc, B-6, and folic acid consumption is poor as well. On average we consume the DRI. But a solid 25 percent of us do not consume this basic level of these nutrients. Our intake of B-12 is much better.

There is an issue that makes the magnesium, iron, and zinc results even worse than they appear from the food survey. Some of our food contains substances that hinder their absorption. You will learn about phytic acid in the grains and legumes chapter and oxalic acid in the fruit and vegetable chapter. You will see that if we are counting on these food groups for our minerals, we need to prepare them properly to maximize our bodies' absorption of them.

Table 6.1: Average intake for women, ages 19 and older 2001–02 NHANES				
Nutrient	Average intake	25th percentile	DRI	How bad?
Magnesium (mg)	240.0	184.0	320.0	Very bad
Iron (mg)	13.1	10.2	18.0	Very bad
Zinc (mg)	9.7	7.5	8.0	Bad
B-6 (mg)	1.5	1.2	1.3	Bad
Folic acid/folate (mcg)	483.0	359.0	400.0	Bad
B-12 (mcg)	4.3	2.8	2.4	Better

All the nutrients in table 6.1 are implicated in depression. Our fat intake is also implicated—low levels of Omega-3 fatty acids are associated with depression. Our intake of this necessary fat is also dreadfully low as you will see.

So, yes, we live in one of the wealthiest parts of the globe with tremendous access to food and to food technology that should keep us healthy. But so far, we have done a very poor job of translating that wealth to our dinner table.

Depression Is on the Rise

We have the tendency in the United States to note the eating habits of the generations following us and scoff. Back in high school, I remember eating a Zinger for lunch and a teacher making a comment along the lines of "kids these days."

"But this is the only time I've eaten a Zinger!" I wanted to exclaim as the teacher walked away. Instead, I just slumped down in my chair.

As an adult I have returned to that same school to do data analysis work and have been shocked at "kids these days." There are children who have a jumbo soda and bag of chips for lunch every day. Their lunch even appears to be somewhat socially acceptable.

Growing rates of disease and obesity among young people have made these lunch time habits the concerns of policy makers. These worsening eating habits have implications for mental health as well.

Rates of depression are increasing with each generation. A cross-national study reported in the *Journal of the American Medical Association* in 1992 found that each new generation is more likely to suffer from depression at some point during its life cycle. Depression is also likely to hit earlier in life. (Cross National Collaborative Group 1992).

In the 2004 National Health Interview Survey, we see that trends continue to worsen. Researchers asked women about their ability to do basic things like carry groceries, visit friends, or enjoy leisure time at home. They then asked a follow-up question: *what condition causes you to have difficulty engaging in these activities?* About 1 percent of respondents mentioned depression. Of those, researchers asked, *how long have you had depression, anxiety, or an emotional problem?*

The younger the respondent was, the more likely she was to have battled with depression. She was also likely to have battled for a longer portion of her life. Women currently in their sixties (my mother's age) have lost an average of 15 percent of their lives to depression—about nine years. Women in my generation, approaching forty, have lost nearly one-third of their lives to depression, also about nine years. Women my age have lived half as many years as women my mother's age and yet we have lost as many years of our lives to depression as our mothers have. Rates are worse still for younger women.

The changing nutrient intake among "kids these days" is likely one player in this picture.

The Nutrient-Depression Link

The human body is complicated and researchers still do not know why, on a fundamental level, we get depressed. Neurotransmitters seem to play a role. Raising the levels of these neurotransmitters in the brain is the goal of popular depression medications—the selective serotonin reuptake inhibitors (SSRIs) and serotonin norepinephrine reuptake inhibitors (SNRIs).

Because depressed people tend to have relatively low levels of serotonin and norepinephrine, the SSRIs and SNRIs work to keep the cells in the brain from reabsorbing these neurotransmitters. They stay locked in the synapses, the spaces between the cells, allowing all the cells to use them as they send signals throughout the brain. The medication essentially raises the brain's levels of neurotransmitters although the whole body's levels are the same.

St. John's Wort also works to block the reuptake of serotonin and is used in complementary medicine in the United States and in mainstream medicine in Europe. Amino acid therapy, the therapy that finally brought me relief, also works to raise your body's levels of neurotransmitters.

The key point for our purposes, however, is that our neurotransmitter levels are also affected by our general nutrient status. Our body uses tryptophan to make serotonin. But in order to do so, it needs vitamin B-6, folate, and magnesium. B-6 also helps convert phenylalanine into tyrosine and tyrosine into norepinephrine. Tyrosine is a common amino acid therapy recommended for depression by alternative medicine doctors because of the importance of phenylalanine and norepinephrine in feeling well. However, in the presence of a B-6 deficiency this amino acid therapy simply will not be effective.

Tyrosine is one of the many supplements I took early on in my depression and it did not do a bit of good even though I had low levels of tyrosine. The reason it was not effective is because I was also deficient in vitamin B-6. In light of a B-6 deficiency, supplemental amino acids will not be effective without added B-6 (which many amino acid blends include).

Regardless of the type of path you use to survive that critical state of depression, look back at your therapy and ask yourself why you needed it. If you used an SSRI, 5HTP, or St. John's Wort, ask yourself why your levels of serotonin were so low in the first place that this therapy was necessary. Do you eat no foods that contain tryptophan? Do you have insufficient amounts of B-6, folate, or magnesium to convert your tryptophan to serotonin? Why is it that you cannot produce these neurotransmitters? It is a basic biological function. Your body should be up to the task if it's working properly.

These are questions one of my doctors asked me when I started on the amino acid therapy. But I was feeling great and I had at least five hundred tasks to catch up on. I was busy and I didn't hear his questions. I had begun a nutrient-rich diet, so I was not concerned about my nutrient intake. I moved on in a state of ignorant bliss without realizing how critical it was to find out why my body was not working properly and not producing all those important neurotransmitters. Yet it is critical for long-term wellness to conduct this search.

FIND THE ANSWERS

My grandmother is the poster child for the need to fix the problem. In the 1940s and 1950s her postpartum depression was treated with shock therapy when she had "nervous breakdowns" and her medication was not sufficient.

Researchers are finding that shock therapy increases the level of zinc in the brain (Nowak et al. 2005). Brain zinc levels are correlated with depression; if you are low in zinc, you are likely to be depressed. My grandmother never treated her zinc deficiency. Well, actually she never had a zinc test, so we don't know for sure that she was deficient. But we do know this: she developed type 2 diabetes at a young age, developed heart problems in her fifties, and died looking very elderly at the age of sixty-one.

We also know that depression and heart problems are associated with low levels of zinc in the body. Researchers are also finding that people suffering from depression benefit from added Omega-3 fatty acids in their diets. People with diabetes or heart disease may benefit from Omega-3s as well. Depression, diabetes, and heart disease share at least one common deficiency: Omega-3 fatty acids. I argue today that my grandmother never fixed the cause of her postpartum depression and she went on to develop other degenerative diseases.

Don't follow that path.

In the next section I provide you with the tools to get to the root of your depression and to go on to live a much healthier life. These are the tools that I have used in my search, tools that depressed people do not have the time or energy to investigate themselves. You will be able to discuss these tools with your doctor and work on improving your quality of life. But before that discussion, let me say something about two controversies that can get in the way of discussing this issue of rebuilding: medication choices and diet choices.

Medication Choices
If you are on or have been on medication for depression, how many times have you felt as though someone who did not use medication judged you to be weak?

If you have not been on antidepressant medication, how many times have you felt as though people have not taken your depression seriously because, after all, you didn't need medication?

You really can't win with either choice.

For my part, I don't care what methods you used to get through that acute period. I am really glad you are here on the other side with the rest of us. Not everyone is as lucky as we are and I wish they had found *anything at all* to change their outcome.

The good news in this book is that whatever your prior choices for therapy, you will benefit by working with your doctor to fix the cause of your problem. In the next section, I refer to studies that use vitamins and minerals in *combination with medication*, so if you are on medication now you can see that there are clinical trials that use both medication and nutritional supplements to help improve the health of the patients in the studies.

Diet Choices

I used to be a vegetarian and was somewhat close to eating no animal products for a while. I became an omnivore because it was the fastest, most efficient way for me to add nutrients to my diet. There is evidence as well that animal fat is necessary in the human diet. The jury is also still out on whether we need animal products for our B-12 and one form of Omega-3 fatty acid (DHA), so I eat animal forms of these nutrients. Others choose the algae forms.

Let's agree to disagree. In this book I discuss strategies to maximize the nutrition in your food. If you are a vegetarian, you will find good tricks to increase the vitamin and mineral content of your plant-based diet. I want people to have the tools to fix the underlying cause of their depression, whatever foods they may choose to eat or avoid.

The Usual Suspects, Your Starting Place

*T*here are a lot of opinions about which nutrients are most important in the depression fight. The reason opinions vary so much is because, at the end of the day, the most important nutrient for you in your depression is the one you are deficient in. So we all need to be mindful of our own circumstances and develop our own plans. However, the medical literature does provide us with a very good place to start.

If you are depressed, you will very likely benefit from additional Omega-3 fatty acids, folate, and vitamin B-12 in your diet. Here is your cheat sheet:

Cheat Sheet

- **Add Omega-3 fatty acids to your diet today.**
  Clinical trials for depression use very large doses of Omega-3 fatty acids. Andrew Stoll in The Omega Connection recommends 4 grams a day of EPA. Most people get added Omega-3 fatty acids by taking a cod liver or fish oil supplement.

- **Add B vitamins to your diet today.**
  The research on the link between folic acid and depression and B-12 and depression is impressive. In clinical trials, depression improves when these nutrients are added to the diet. There is some evidence as well for the importance of vitamin B-6 and historically clinicians have used niacin (vitamin B-3). Add a good B vitamin supplement to your diet.

Read on for more detail.

Omega-3 Fatty Acids

It is becoming increasingly accepted that correcting deficiencies in Omega-3 fatty acids is therapeutic for depression. Omega-3 supplements line the shelves and refrigerators of health food stores. Short articles about Omega-3s cover the Internet. Often the information we receive is simply "increase your Omega-3s." I was told to consume one tablespoon of cod liver oil a day for the depression and was directed to a national brand carried at Whole Foods and many other health food stores. Nearly every day for three years I took a tablespoon of that particular cod liver oil. Some days I took two tablespoons.

The problem with this approach is that not all tablespoons contain the same dosage of the Omega-3 oil. It was not until I read the works of Andrew L. Stoll, *The Omega-3 Connection: The Groundbreaking Omega-3 Antidepression Diet* and *Brain Program*, that I realized how deficient both my pregnancy diet and my postnatal cod liver oil supplementation, given my struggle with depression.

Stoll discusses the limitations of our modern diet in the context of Omega-3 fatty acids. Whereas our ancestors received much of their Omega-3s from fish and game, our sources of fish and meat tend to have much lower levels of Omega-3 fatty acids. Traditionally wild fish fed on algae, high in Omega-3s, and the fat in their bodies contained high levels of Omega-3s. Wild game, free to graze on their natural diets of grasses and clover, were less fat overall and had much higher levels of Omega-3s. When our ancestors fished or hunted and consumed these animals, they consumed much higher levels of Omega-3s, levels at a 1:1 ratio with their cousins the Omega-6 fatty acids.

Meats grown commercially in this country are higher in Omega-6 and lower in Omega-3 fatty acids than was the traditional human diet. As we eat these food sources, our diets become deficient in Omega-3s. Stoll reports that the Omega-6 to Omega-3 ratio in the modern diet is approximately 20:1 compared to about 1:1 in the Paleolithic diet of many generations past.

Stoll makes a compelling argument for high doses of Omega-3 fatty acids as therapeutic for depression, particularly eicosapentaenoic acid (EPA), one type of Omega-3 fatty acid. He makes the point that researchers are not clear on why Omega-3s fight depression, but they are important in so many biological processes such as cell building and brain function that there may be many reasons a deficient diet impacts our moods.

The Omega-3 Depression Link

Research on Omega-3 fatty acids and depression has found the following:

- People with depression tend to have low levels of Omega-3s in their blood or a high Omega-6 to Omega-3 ratio (Tiemeier et al. 2003).
- In controlled clinical trials, dosages of about 10 grams per day of EPA have been shown to be effective in treating depression (Su et al. 2003; Stoll et al. 1999). However, one study found that only 1 gram/day was effective in patients who were taking antidepressant medication but were still depressed (Peet et al. 2002).
- Controlled trials combine antidepressant medication with Omega-3 fatty acids for improved results (Su et al. 2003; Nemets et al. 2002; Peet et al. 2002).
- Patients tend to see positive results in two to eight weeks (Su et al. 2003).
- Postpartum depression clinical trials are in their infancy. The findings have been inconclusive but they have had problematic study designs. A 2004 study examined seven pregnant women with a history of depression and had inconclusive results with supplementation of 3 grams of DHA+EPA (Marangell et al. 2004). A 2003 study selected pregnant women, did not consider their depression history, and supplemented with a very small dosage of docosahexaenoic acid (DHA)—200 mg/day or a placebo (Llorente et al. 2003). Both EPA and DHA are Omega-3 fatty acids.

The research on general depression has found EPA supplementation to alleviate depression, but in the postpartum case, researchers speculate that DHA is important since DHA is required for the baby's growing brain. At this point, we do not know which Omega-3 fatty acid matters most in the postpartum case.

Added Stress of Pregnancy and Breastfeeding

Clinical trials on postpartum moms are in their infancy, but we have strong theoretical reason to believe that Omega-3 fatty acids are critical to our mental health. First, the clinical trials on major depression give us good reason to believe that Omega-3 fatty acids help with depression. Second, at no time in life may Omega-3 fatty acids be as important as they are in pregnancy and breastfeeding.

As the baby develops in utero, DHA is needed for brain development. Mother's milk contains high levels of DHA to meet the baby's early needs for DHA in infancy. The baby is first in line for this nutrient and so any amount of DHA and EPA that the baby needs is taken from mom's blood levels. If mom's diet is deficient and her blood levels are low, the baby might take fatty acids from the Omega-3 stores in mom's tissues. In this way, a baby can literally deplete an already fairly depleted mom of her Omega-3 stores.

A key dietary source of Omega-3 fatty acids is fish. In his 2001 article, Hibbeln examines the relationship between postpartum depression and fish consumption at the national level. In twenty-three countries he estimates levels of postpartum depression from the research other scholars have done in each of those countries. He compares these estimated levels of postpartum depression to the levels of fish consumed (measured by national catches plus imports minus exports) and shows a compelling relationship between the two. Low levels of fish consumption are associated with higher levels of postpartum depression. Fish consumption may be the first line of attack against postpartum depression.

Very, Very Common Deficiency

When it comes to Omega-3 fatty acids, the question is, who are the few people around you who are actually getting enough? Our need for EPA and DHA is so great in pregnancy and during breastfeeding, but most of us simply do not consume enough.

A Canadian study followed the diet of twenty pregnant women who did not know the topic of study. Researchers analyzed food samples and measured blood levels of fatty acids. Of those twenty women, eighteen of them (90 percent) consumed less than the 300 mg per day of DHA as recommended by the International Society for the Study of Fatty Acids and Lipids Working Group (Denomme et al. 2005; Innis and Elias 2003). Keep in mind that the 300 mg per day is low if you are battling depression.

How to Test

You can have blood drawn to test the level of various fatty acids in your blood. A national lab called Metametrix will provide you with a long list of fats found in your blood or in your red blood cells. But if you are short on cash, you can begin by simply analyzing your diet. My Web site has additional information on Omega-3 fatty acids in foods.

Are You a Quart Low?

As I have added cod liver oil to my diet, my chronic chapped lips and dry skin have disappeared. In the winters now I manage my dry skin with a weekly or biweekly application of olive oil on my legs and arms and I use a lip balm on occasion. In the past, I used lotion on my arms and legs multiple times each day and they were still dry. I carried lip balm with me all the time so that my overly chapped lips would not hurt as much. I've come a long way because of these dietary fats.

Our body uses the fats to build our skin cells, just as it uses them to build cells throughout our body. My skin is not only hydrated, but it is softer and smoother than I ever remember it. If your skin is dry and cracking, oil on the inside is far more effective than oil on the outside. Beneficial oil in your diet gives your body the tools to make soft, smooth skin. Add fish oil to your diet today and you may find that not only is your depression alleviated, but your skin feels better than ever.

Toxicities of Omega-3s are unlikely. For most of us it will verge on the impossible to get our diets anywhere near the ideal ratio of 1:1 of Omega-6 to Omega-3. In the case of pyroluria (see inset article in the B-6 section on

Omega-3s for Vegetarians

EPA and DHA are found only in animal products but are critical in the fight against postpartum depression. In *The Omega Connection*, Stoll recommends flaxseed oil for those allergic to fish or those on a vegetarian diet. Flaxseed oil contains alpha linolenic acid (ALA), which the body can convert to EPA. It is not known the degree to which the human body can adequately convert ALA to EPA but there is some evidence that it can (Harper et al. 2006).

However, pregnant and breastfeeding moms should seek out sources of DHA, not just ALA. DHA is necessary for baby's brain development and baby acquires it from mom in the third trimester and during breastfeeding. Studies of lactating women have found that the ALA in flaxseed oil *does not* convert to DHA (Francois et al. 2003; de Groot et al. 2004). The best sources of DHA that fit the vegetarian lifestyle are non-fertile eggs from free-range hens. Eggs from caged hens fed no flax seed or fish-related feed are insignificant sources of DHA. Algae sources of DHA are also available online for those who consume no animal products.

page 81), Omega-3s may aggravate depression. In general, consult with your doctor on your specific dosage and work to add Omega-3 foods to your diet and to reduce unhealthy fats, particularly partially hydrogenated oils (trans fats).

If you are a quart low, add Omega-3s to your diet to avoid some problems that may be associated with a low Omega-3 status:

- Alzheimer's (Alessandri et al. 2004)
- cardiovascular disease (Breslow 2006)
- rheumatoid arthritis (Simopoulos 2002)
- multiple sclerosis (Simopoulos 2002)
- diabetes (Ebbesson et al. 2005)

Dietary Sources

In the food chapters of this book you will find many sources of Omega-3 fatty acids. The standouts are wild-caught fatty fish, cod liver oil, and fish oil.

Stoll recommends flaxseed oil for alpha linolenic acid (ALA), which the body can convert to EPA to some degree.

But there is a flip side to the coin here: while you are increasing your intake of Omega-3 fatty acids, reduce your intake of Omega-6 fatty acids as well to reduce your Omega-6 to Omega-3 fatty acid ratio. I discuss this balance between Omega-6 and Omega-3 fatty acids in the food chapters that follow.

The B-Vitamin Family

At an appointment with our chiropractor some years ago, he told me that the color of my lips betrayed my poor B vitamin status.

"Look at your lips! They have no color!" he said.

"That's right, he's got my lip color!" I said, pointing to my son Frederick.

Frederick has beautiful red lips. I am pleased that I had enough B vitamins to give him a decent B vitamin storage, even though I didn't have enough for the both of us.

I've looked for research on our chiropractor's claim but have found none yet. However, I notice the other children at preschool. Their lips do tend to be darker than their moms' lips. Babies in utero receive our nutrients preferentially. That is, they are first in line for whatever nutrients our bodies are absorbing from our food. If our own diets are inadequate or our digestion poor, our lips may become increasingly pale as we give our stores to our children.

In that case, our own bodies struggle with an ever-diminishing supply of B vitamins and one typical response of our bodies is depression. The whole B vitamin family is implicated in depression, but the most thoroughly researched B vitamins are B-12 and folic acid. However, vitamins B-6 and B-3 (niacin) are commonly used by practitioners who are treating depression with nutrients.

Vitamin B-12

This book has been an emotional book to research and write because I come across data constantly on babies deprived of nutrition in utero. Moms try hard to eat well while pregnant, but we miss the mark on occasion. Vitamin B-12 is an example.

In those last two months of gestation we begin to give B-12 to our children. If they make an early arrival, they likely have not received their full inheritance. In a sick twist of fate, they are actually more likely to make an early arrival if we are deficient in B-12 (Vollset et al. 2000). And as we breastfeed them, the levels in the milk we make relate to the levels in our blood. If our blood levels are low, so too are the levels in our breast milk (Chanarin 1999, p 1428).

The rich get richer and the poor get poorer.

We have at least three generations of nutritional poverty in my family. I mention my own maternal grandmother throughout this book and I have suggested that my mother inherited postpartum depression from her. It is an easy argument to make, really: Grandmother bequeathed her vitamin and mineral stores to my mother who bequeathed an ever-dwindling supply to me. My grandmother did not even have the courtesy to pass on her movie star good looks as part of the package. But her body had no choice but to pass on a poor supply of B vitamins.

B-12 and Depression

It is not surprising, then, that depression tends to run in families. Researchers find that you are more likely to be depressed if your parents were depressed (Kendler et al. 1986). But we also know that a baby born to a B-12 deficient mother is likely to be B-12 deficient. While there may be a genetic factor in depression, there is also an issue of nutritional inheritance given the critical role of B vitamins in the depression fight. Researchers have found that those of us who tend to be depressed also tend to be:

- low in B-12 (Penninx et al. 2000)

- high in homocysteine, a marker of a B-12, folic acid, or B-6 deficiency (Coppen and Bolander-Gouaille 2005)

Researchers suggest that B-12 and folic acid are crucial because of their role in creating S-adenosylmethionine (SAMe) in the body (Coppen and Bolander-Gouaille 2005). SAMe is made from the amino acid methionine, but B-12 and folic acid are crucial in the process. SAMe has become a popular treatment for depression.

Deficiency Signs
A B-12 deficiency can result from a diet low in B-12 or from malabsorption problems that keep your body from recycling its own B-12. Strict vegetarians who eat no animal products are at most risk for a B-12 deficiency since B-12 is found only in animal products.

You can walk for a long time on this earth with a deficiency in vitamin B-12 and not realize it. There are no specific clinical signs in the intermediate stages. Your best bet is to shore up your diet or to supplement with an animal-based B-12 supplement if you do not want to consume animal-based foods (see my argument in "Dietary Sources" below).

You doctor can test your blood levels of B-12. The normal range for a plasma cobalamin test is greater than 200 pg/ml. However, the range is controversial and your doctor may direct you to supplement your B-12 if you are under 500. Many doctors prefer to test first your plasma homocysteine level, an indirect measure of low B-12, folate, or B-6. If your plasma homocysteine is elevated, then you can work with your doctor to determine if you are deficient in B-12, folate, B-6, or some combination of the three.

Do take the time to investigate which of these B vitamins may be your biggest culprits. A problem with the "more is better" approach or a wild shot gun approach to supplementation is provided to us by the folic acid supplementation in the United States. Researchers are finding that supplemental folic acid will help your cognitive function if you have sufficient levels of vitamin B-12. If you are low in B-12, supplemental folic acid will actually impede your brain function (Morris et al. 2007).

B-12, Folic Acid, and Antidepressants:
Supplementing improves the effectiveness of medication

Researchers are finding that patients deficient in B-12 and/or folic acid have improved treatment on their antidepressant medication if they are also supplementing this deficiency. Coppen and Bolander-Gouaille (2005) reviewed the studies on depression and vitamin B-12 and folic acid and found that low levels of each are related to a poor response to antidepressants. Supplementing folate or B-12 in the diet helped patients respond better to their medication. Fava et al. (1997) found that patients with folic acid deficiencies were less likely to respond to fluoxetine (Prozac) in a double-blind placebo study. In their 1990 study published in the *Lancet*, Godfrey and colleagues found that 33 percent of the patients in their study were deficient in folate. 15 mg/day of methylfolate improved their clinical outcomes in a double-blind placebo study. Procter (1991) also found that in patients with low folate, medication therapy was more effective with the supplementation of folic acid.

Dietary Sources of B-12

At the lowest end of the food chain, B-12 is produced in algae and eaten by small fish that are nourished by the B-12. Larger fish eat those fish and take in the B-12. Bears and seals eat those larger B-12-filled fish. Historically, humans hunted those bears and seals and thereby met our B-12 requirements.

With the exception of the algae, there are no vegetable foods that contain B-12, making B-12 problematic for the vegan diet. Furthermore, there is evidence that the algae form of vitamin B-12 is a B-12 analog, an inactive form for humans (Herbert 1988). Highly committed vegans will disagree because there is some evidence that some of the B-12 in algae is active and that it is theoretically possible to get your B-12 from this plant source (Takenaka et al. 2001). Further, there are stories of vegans who have lived long lives without supplementing their B-12. Indeed, research shows that people can live twenty to thirty years without B-12 in their diet if their bodies have no absorption problems (Herbert 1987) and perhaps longer if they had excellent liver stores. As those years pass, their liver stores dwindle.

If you are a woman and still having children, keep in mind that your extra B-12 is stored in your liver and you will bequeath those liver stores to your children. If your liver stores are good, the liver stores of your children are also likely to be good and, particularly if you have boys, those boys might be able to live a long, vegan life without B-12 supplementation. But as you continue to have babies and if you are B-12 deficient, your subsequent children will inherit an ever-depleted B-12 store from you. You will also face increased health consequences. I do not recommend algae forms of B-12 as a sole source of B-12 because there is too much evidence that much of the B-12 in algae is inactive. I appreciate the vegetarian ethic, but I hope that vegans can make one exception by including an animal-based B-12 in the diet, particularly if they are in their childbearing years.

As a side note, if most of your B-12 comes from algae sources and you get your blood tested for cobalamin (B-12), it will measure the active and inactive forms floating around inside you. It will give you a false sense of security. A plasma homocysteine test will be a better measure for you because it will give you a sense of the functional amount of B-12 in your body. If your levels are at all elevated (above 8), consider a methylmalonic acid (MMA) test. If your levels are elevated, consider an animal-based supplement.

An additional factor in the B-12 story is that your body needs to be producing a protein called intrinsic factor (IF) in order for your dietary B-12 to be absorbed. People suffering from an IF deficiency need to work with their doctors to get adequate B-12 supplementation through injections or sublingual tablets.

Nature's top B-12 sources include:

- **Liver** is your best bet for those willing to eat anything to increase their levels of B-12. I provide recipes in the meat chapter.
- **Clams** and **oysters** are at the top of the USDA's list of B-12 rich foods as well.

Vitamin C, Folate, and Iron

Vitamin C is important for the depression fight in part because our bodies need it to use our folate. It also helps us absorb the iron in our food. It is a nutrient most sensitive to heat loss and storage. An orange, for instance, filled with vitamin C, will lose some of that vitamin C as it sits, will lose it more quickly once it is juiced, and it will all but disappear if it is cooked.

Find fresh food high in vitamin C and eat it raw or preserve it with traditional fermentation techniques to maintain its vitamin C content.

Sore and bleeding gums are an early sign of low vitamin C. As scurvy develops, the gums may ulcerate and your teeth may fall out.

FOLATE

Folate deficiency is so common that folic acid is now added to grain-based processed foods in the United States. Most of us do not get enough folate from our foods and many of us do not even get enough folic acid from our enriched grain products, as we saw in the previous chapter. Low folate intake can lead to a folate deficiency.

Deficiency Signs

A sore red tongue and slow growth are signs of low folate. A plasma homocysteine test may be the most efficient first test to request from your doctor. A high homocysteine level (above 8) would suggest a possible deficiency in folate, B-12, or B-6. A red blood cell folate test would then be your next step. This measures folate levels over the last three months as opposed to a serum level, which reflects recent dietary folate intake. If you eat meals high in folate prior to a serum folate test, you may have a normal test despite having low liver stores of folate. Low folate can also result in anemia. Do not overlook folate as one possible cause of low hemoglobin.

Folate and Depression

The evidence for the folate-depression link is mounting. If you are low in folate, you are likely to be depressed (Fava et al. 1997; Bottinglieri 1990). If you are high in homocysteine (a marker of a folic acid deficiency) you are likely to be depressed (Coppen and Bolander-Gouaille 2005). In clinical trials where patients were given vitamins to treat their depression, researchers found that:

- Depressed patients improved with folic acid (Coppen and Bailey 2000).
- Folic-acid deficient patients improved if they supplemented with folic acid (Godfrey et al. 1990).

Dietary Sources

A key reason most of us do not consume enough folate in our diets is because we do not eat enough fruit and vegetables, we do not eat them fresh enough, and we tend to cook them. Besides liver and kidney (the organ meats of animals), folate is found most commonly in dark leafy greens. But if those greens sit for a couple of days at room temperature, they may lose 50 percent or more of their folate. When we cook them, they could lose an additional 50 percent and upwards of 100 percent of their folate. You need to make a concerted effort to add folate to your diet by adding fresh leafy greens to your diet (and liver and kidney if you are more adventuresome).

Folate Supplements and Nutrient Interactions

Coppen and Bolander-Gouaille (2005) recommend dietary supplementation of 800 mg/day of folic acid. However, doses of 350 mg or more of supplemental folic acid can reduce your ability to absorb zinc (Herbert 1987). If you face a major zinc deficiency, you might want to increase your dietary folate, not supplemental vitamin folic acid, while you rebuild your body's zinc.

Vitamins, Minerals, and Probiotics

Probiotics are food supplements that contain beneficial bacteria and yeast to help re-establish a good balance of bacteria and yeast in your intestinal tract. Antibiotic use and consumption of refined foods can throw off the natural balance of beneficial microbes in your intestines. A telltale sign in women of an imbalance is a vaginal yeast infection. Thrush during breastfeeding is another.

Re-establishing a good balance is critical in the depression fight. First, overgrowth of bad bacteria will impede your digestion of B vitamins. Those bad bacteria have to live on something and your B vitamins are their food of choice. Second, you will improve your mineral absorption as you increase the beneficial microbes in your intestinal tract (Van Loo et al. 1999).

But you do not have to buy an expensive food supplement to aid your digestion. Nature provides us with probiotics in the form of cultured and fermented food. Natural fermentation of food increases the lactic acid in that food and that lactic acid will help you absorb the nutrients in your food. A study of milk, cultured versus not cultured, found that calcium was absorbed more in the cultured milk (Rasic 1987). Eat yogurt, drink kefir, and ferment your fruits and vegetables. I provide directions in the Appendix.

Vitamin B-6

Many of us are deficient in vitamin B-6. Studies of B-6 have found large percentages of the population deficient, particularly those of us in our childbearing years:

- 68 percent of low-income pregnant women are deficient in B-6 (Schuster et al. 1981).
- 42 percent of pregnant women are deficient (Heller et al. 1973).
- 13 percent of pregnant adolescents are deficient (Martner-Hewes et al. 1986).

These B-6 studies are decades old in some cases, some from back in my high school days. In my day in high school, students had not yet fully perfected

Pyroluria

If you find that you exhibit signs of deficiencies in B-6 and zinc, consider getting a urine test for pyroluria. People with pyroluria produce too many pyrroles. Pyrroles bind to B-6 and zinc and then, together, they are excreted out in the urine. People with pyroluria are treated with higher levels of B-6 and zinc than are those without the condition because they simply have a much higher need for these nutrients. The lab work is about $50. I provide labs in the Appendix.

the soda pop and big-bag-of-chips lunch that is common today. The fact is, a good number of us have been deficient for some time. With current dietary practices, those numbers cannot be getting better.

B-6 Depression Link

B-6 is necessary for your body to convert amino acids into key neurotransmitters. Several studies found that supplemental B-6 improves depression (Adams et al. 1973; Bell 1992; Doll 1989) and that B-6 deficiency is correlated with depression (Hvas et al. 2004). However, not all studies have been able to replicate the link (Lerner et al. 2002).

But do not let mixed findings in the medical literature discourage you. The peculiar point about B-6 clinical trials is that researchers do not tend to select participants who are low in B-6. They simply select anyone who is depressed. If you are not getting adequate B-6 in your diet, you need to improve your intake and your depression may just improve as well.

Deficiency Signs

You are already adding the whole B vitamin family to your diet but you may find reason to focus more on vitamin B-6. The key question is whether you need more.

- You can have your blood tested. The most common test used is the blood plasma test for pyriodoxal 5-phosphate (P5P).

- You can look at your body. One important bit of wisdom for identifying B-6 deficiencies comes out of the Brain Bio Center from the work of Carl Pfeiffer and his colleagues, who worked for years on the link between nutrients and depression. In 1973 Pfeiffer and his colleagues discovered that people deficient in B-6 were unable to recall their dreams. Pfeiffer argues that it is normal for people to be able to recall their last dream each night. He supplemented patients with B-6 until they began to do so.
- You can examine your diet. Keep a food journal for about a week and examine your B-6 intake.

If you are taking large amounts of B-6 or P5P, take it in the morning. For most vitamins, spreading the dosage throughout the day will maximize your body's ability to absorb the vitamin. That is the case here as well, but B-6 will also cause you to urinate more. It could interrupt your sleep if you were taking large doses later in the day.

See the Appendix for information on B-6 tests and dosages.

Dietary Sources

B-6 is one of those vitamins found much more densely in animal products than in plants. Vegetarians need to establish extra diligence to get enough B-6 in their diets. Some stand-outs:

- Beef liver. As with the other B vitamins, the liver stores B-6 to help in its detoxification process. This storage place for B-6 gives us an opportunity to load up on B vitamins in our diets.
- Other food sources are chestnuts, buckwheat, poultry, and halibut.

MOTIVATION TO FIX YOUR B-VITAMIN STATUS

A study published in 2000 in the *American Journal of Clinical Nutrition* provides us with some great motivation to fix these deficiencies. Vollset et al. analyzed plasma homocysteine levels and found that elevated levels (an indirect measure of deficiencies in B-12, B-6, or folic acid) increase the **risk in pregnancy** of the following:

- preeclampsia
- premature birth
- low birth weight
- stillbirth
- neural tube defect
- club foot

High plasma homocysteine levels are also associated with heart disease and stroke. You need to fix the problem today, particularly if you are a woman who plans to have more children. See the Appendix for more information on lab tests for B-12 and folate.

More Investigation:
Additional Nutrients

*A*ny nutrient deficiency you have is likely to worsen your depression, but the purpose of this book is to help us focus on some of the more likely suspects so that we can get some relief. You are already working on your Omega-3 fatty acids and your B vitamins. Keep working on them. But what other nutrients do we need to worry about? This is a more difficult question because the answer really depends upon your specific nutrient status.

In this chapter, I will address three additional nutrients in detail: magnesium, zinc, and iron. What you do not want to do with the information in this chapter is just take all the nutrients I list as supplements. If you do not need zinc, for instance, it can have toxic consequences. You do not need new problems. Your challenge will be determining which, if any, of these nutrients you need. You can begin your investigation by examining your blood, your body, and your diet.

EXAMINE YOUR NUTRIENT STATUS

Blood work will be your best in examining your nutrient status, though all tests are surrounded in their controversies. If you have the funds, get these tests:

- red blood cell mineral panel (see Appendix)
- a ferritin test for iron (see iron section, page 92)

I provide labs for the red blood cell panel in the Appendix. Your doctor's regular labs will not provide access to these tests for all the nutrients I describe in this chapter, but your doctor can start an account with these companies and order the tests for you.

The red blood cell panel costs in the neighborhood of $500. It is a high cost, but it will reduce a great deal of guesswork. Without a panel, you can still examine body signs and your dietary intake.

You can also examine your body. Deficiencies in the three minerals in this chapter come with body signs. If you have these body signs, talk to your doctor about specific tests for them and add these nutrients to your diet.

- **Zinc.** If you have slow growing hair and nails, white spots on your finger nails, or are prone to stretch marks, read the section in this chapter on zinc.
- **Magnesium.** If your muscles twitch and jerk, if you have charley horses or leg cramps, read the section on magnesium.
- **Iron.** If you have little energy and little color in your face, dizziness, or shortness of breath, read the section on iron.

It is also a good idea to keep a food diary and determine the nutrient content of the food you typically eat. Visit my Web site for resources on calculating the nutrient content of your meals. Determine what you may not be getting in your diet. If you suspect you are low in zinc, magnesium, or iron, read on.

ZINC

Zinc was not one of the deficiencies on my radar before I became pregnant. But compared to the traditional meat based diet of our ancestors, the diet for most of my life was fairly low in zinc. And apparently, I am not alone: in a 1994–96 survey of American diets, approximately 80 percent of women between the ages of twenty and forty did not consume the DRI of zinc.

We can expect zinc deficiencies to increase if diets continue on their current path. Traditional sources of zinc are meat-based foods. With a shift toward vegetable protein in grains and legumes, the American diet as a whole contains lower levels of zinc than did the traditional diet. Whole grains do contain zinc, but they also contain phytates which bind to the zinc and keep it from being absorbed (Egli et al. 2004). If you consume a lot of grains and legumes and very few animal products, you are likely absorbing far less zinc than you realize. I discuss phytates in detail in the chapter on grains and legumes and provide suggestions to help you increase your mineral absorption.

Deficiency Signs

Zinc provides us with some visual clues if we are deficient. Zinc is important in the growth of our fingernails and hair and our body provides us with some signs:

- soft or thin fingernails
- white spots on fingernails
- slow hair growth

Our children may also provide us with some signs of a zinc deficiency. Our own children are often a good mirror into our nutritional status. Whenever I meet a woman who has a young child with health or behavioral problems aggravated by nutrition and she is wondering how to supplement that child, yet the child is still breastfeeding, I discuss her diet primarily and only then the solid foods in the child's diet. Breast milk is a powerful vehicle for child nutrition in a mom who has the nutrients flowing through her body anyway.

Zinc-deficient children tend to be small. I know we are not supposed to worry about the size of our children, but it is a sign of zinc status. Zinc is necessary for tissue growth, and mild zinc deficiencies can retard growth. In a fascinating zinc study, researchers gathered a group of infants and toddlers, apparently healthy, who were small for their age. They gave them 5 milligrams of zinc over a six-month period and those children outgrew the children in the study not receiving zinc (Walravens et al. 1989). Researchers concluded that a mild zinc deficiency was one of the factors in children failing to thrive. The study design and results suggests an important point for us:

- Small children may be small because they are mildly zinc deficient.

And the small-child finding suggests something important for moms:

- Children who are zinc deficient, fed in the same homes as their moms (and possibly breastfed as well by that mom), suggest a mom who is zinc deficient.

Read more about zinc testing in the Appendix.

Zinc and Depression

If you are deficient in zinc, it is likely contributing to your depression:

- **Low levels of zinc are correlated with depression** (Maes 1994; Nowak et al. 2005).
- **The lower the zinc levels, the worse the depression.** One study found that patients with lower serum zinc also tended to have major depression and those with intermediate zinc levels (borderline) tended to have minor depression (Maes et al. 1994).
- **Clinical trials improve depression.** In a double-blind and placebo-controlled study, patients felt better after six weeks if they were also taking zinc supplements (Nowak et al. 2003).
- **Zinc can complement antidepressant therapy.** Patients in the Nowak et al. 2003 study were also on antidepressant medication. The zinc therapy improved their depression above the relief provided by the medication.
- You might be able to **increase your brain zinc levels** very quickly, today, if you have **shock therapy.** Nowak et al. (2005) find that shock therapy increases brain levels of zinc in the rat brain. But this is not a great strategy either since it doesn't fix the underlying zinc problem in the longer term.

Dietary Sources

Zinc is found most densely in the animal world, particularly in:

- oysters
- beef
- turkey
- crab
- lamb
- duck

Vegetarians tend to rely on grains and legumes for zinc, but only about 15 percent of that zinc will be useable to your body. That percentage will be closer to 10 percent if the food source is a high-phytate, low-phytase food like soy, which you will learn about in the grain and legume chapter.

More Motivation to Fix Your Zinc

Mothering gives us many incentives to fix our own health problems. In the animal world, researchers have found that pregnant animals with zinc deficiencies have difficult deliveries and display abnormal behavior towards their babies (e.g., they are more likely to ignore them). Their babies do not learn as well as comparable babies who are not zinc deficient (Vallee and Falchuk 1993).

In the human world, low zinc is related to:

- premature births (Scholl et al. 1993)
- low-birth-weight babies (Scholl et al. 1993)
- intrauterine growth retardation (Goldenberg et al. 1995)
- congenital abnormalities in baby such as spina bifida (Keen and Hurley 1989)
- rheumatoid arthritis (Vallee and Falchuk 1993)
- heart conditions (Reiterer 2005)

Vitamin D and Seasonal Affective Disorder

Low levels of vitamin D have been implicated in seasonal affective disorder (SAD). Our body produces vitamin D from exposure to sunlight. During the winter in the northern hemisphere, we have fewer hours of sunlight, we keep our skin covered, and we tend to stay inside. Less sunlight means a lower vitamin status. Clinical trials of vitamin D and depression have not found a strong link, though it is certainly compelling that vitamin D is implicated in SAD.

To test your vitamin D levels, ask your doctor for the 25-hydroxyvitamin D test.

Even if you are borderline low in vitamin D, add seafood, egg yolks, and cod liver oil to your diet to improve your vitamin D levels. If you can ensure some regular sunlight throughout the year, your body will be able to make vitamin D. But you can get too much of a good thing here too: high intake of vitamin D (particularly from nutritional supplements) could lead to high levels of vitamin D and high levels of calcium.

Visit http://www.sunlightandvitamind.com for more information.

MAGNESIUM

I reflect on my lifelong magnesium deficiency. Back in high school I played in the band as a percussionist. I played the bells, an instrument one octave short of a xylophone. The instrument weighed about 30 pounds and I harnessed it on my back for parades and halftime shows. I was fourteen years old and my muscle mass was not all that could be hoped for, thanks in large part to my continual yo-yo dieting. The instrument was manageable but a bit of a strain. Our most important parade of the year was a 5-mile parade and we would be judged at various points along the way. It was an invitation-only parade, so we felt pretty proud to be in it and felt the pressure to march and play well.

The night before the parade I woke up in the middle of the night with a whopper of a charley horse. Charley horses are those sudden muscle spasms, usually at night, where your muscle tightens up and burns. It was my right calf muscle that night and I worked out the spasm so that I could get back to sleep. The next morning in the parade the pain lingered in that calf. Ironically, marching and carrying the bells was much less painful than standing in an at-ease position. I can remember standing at ease with my calf flexed backwards praying for the drum major to command us to march. The muscle pain continued for another day or two.

Throughout my pregnancy my leg would jerk in the middle of the night in an uncontrollable spasm. It would wake me and sometimes wake my husband. My muscles twitched in various places, including near my temple. I lived through my whole pregnancy magnesium deficient. Heck, I lived through my teens and my twenties magnesium deficient.

Deficiency Signs
A key sign of magnesium deficiency is muscle spasms and twitching. A rapid heartbeat, confusion, and nausea are signs of low magnesium. There are some physical tests your doctor can perform for low magnesium that I provide in the Appendix.

Magnesium and Depression
And those spasms and twitches matter in the depression fight:

- Low body levels of magnesium are associated with **suicidal behavior** (Banki et al. 1985).
- **Suicide victims** have low magnesium levels in their cerebrospinal fluid, an indirect measure of brain levels of magnesium (Singewald et al. 2004).
- **Magnesium-deficient mice get depressed** (Singewald et al. 2004).

Sherry Rogers, a clinician who treats depression with vitamins, minerals, and other natural remedies and author of *Depression: Cured at Last*, argues that in some patients, magnesium deficiency is the primary cause of depression. Fixing the magnesium fixes the depression entirely. In *The Miracle of Magnesium*, clinician Carolyn Dean discusses alleviating depression in her patients with magnesium therapy.

Your doctor can test your magnesium levels with a red blood cell magnesium test but it is possible to be low in magnesium and still have normal red blood cell or serum levels. See the Appendix for additional information.

Keeping Your Head Above Water

Depression is all about keeping your head above water. On bad days it is often all you can do to survive the day doing only the minimal activity required. Forget about outings, forget about shopping, forget about moving the garden hose. Survive the day. Keep your head above water. When the day is over and you have not drowned, it was a "win." You survived.

Mice and rats must be a lot like humans. Their ability to fit in the smallest crack in my kitchen cabinets aside, when mice are depressed, all they can do is keep their heads above water.

In depression studies of mice, researchers literally throw them into a water tank and observe them swimming. Healthy mice meet the challenge and swim. Depressed mice may swim at first but they will soon wear out and the only movements they will make in that tank of water are the minimal movements necessary to keep their heads above water.

Dietary Sources

Whole grain cereals are a good source of magnesium, if you have prepared them properly to break down the phytic acid using methods I discuss in the grain and legume chapter. Other good sources of magnesium include:

- kelp
- green leafy vegetables
- molasses
- nuts, particularly almonds
- brewer's yeast

More Motivation to Rebuild Your Magnesium

Magnesium is implicated in many unpleasantries:

- asthma (Jong and Rud 2005)
- attention deficit disorder (Starobrat-Hermelin and Kozielec 1997)
- preeclampsia (Jong and Rud 2005)
- pancreatitis (Papazachariou et al. 2000)
- chronic fatigue syndrome (Cox et al. 1991)

Iron

Women who have been pregnant receive fair warning from obstetricians and midwives that they need to watch their iron intake. Hemoglobin levels get monitored in pregnancy. And though the poking and prodding gets old if you are the pregnant woman, the importance of iron in pregnancy and in nutrition in general cannot be overstated. We saw in the previous chapter that the average woman does not consume nearly enough iron in a day. Add pregnancy to the picture, where her body is required to produce more blood to support the uterine lining and placenta, and iron deficiencies become quite common. As she gets older, she is increasingly likely to be low in iron, particularly after the age of seventy, regardless of her pregnancy status in those early years.

The Western diet is in a large part responsible for our low iron status. Foods low in iron such as white flour and potato chips have replaced higher iron whole foods such as whole wheat bread and legumes. Meat consumption has been on the decline as well, which would be a good source of iron in an otherwise processed-food diet.

Deficiency Signs

My friend Jennifer, who had record-breaking low levels of iron, was plagued by common signs of the deficiency: pale coloring and exhaustion. After only about two months of iron supplementation, a friend she had not seen in a few months looked at her and said, "You have color in your face, my dear!"

If your skin is pale, if you are fatigued, if you chill easily, if your heart beats rapidly, if you are prone to dizziness, if your fingers and toes tingle, you might be low in iron.

Iron and Depression

The focus in research on iron and depression is on postpartum depression. At no other time in life is the iron requirement for a woman so great as during pregnancy and breastfeeding. It is difficult to meet our iron requirement in pregnancy and, depending on the iron stores we entered the pregnancy with, we could end up iron deficient and perhaps with anemia (below normal levels of red blood cells or hemoglobin). Research finds that treating an iron deficiency will also improve our depression.

- A study of ninety-five new mothers in South Africa found that treating iron deficiency anemia with an iron supplement (125 mg of ferrous sulfate) improved the mood of the mothers (Beard et al. 2005)
- New mothers in Pennsylvania were more likely to be depressed if they were low in iron (Corwin et al. 2003).

Dietary Sources

Your body will tend to absorb more iron from meat sources. The standouts for iron in the meat world are crab and organ meats such as liver. In the plant world, select some of the more unusual grains such as quinoa, amaranth, and millet, and legumes such as soy and lentils, and follow my preparation tips in the grains and legumes chapter. You will absorb more iron if your meal includes vitamin C, so add tomato, fruit, or other sources of vitamin C to your meal. Milk tends to inhibit iron absorption in other foods, so it is best to eat your high-iron meals with limited dairy foods. Visit my Web site for a free e-book about food and iron.

More Motivation to Rebuild Your Iron

People low in iron need little motivation to fix the problem. Fixing the exhaustion that accompanies low iron is surely reason enough to attend to the problem. But nature gives us more motivation:

- Low iron impairs your thyroid metabolism (Zimmerman 2006).
- Low iron impairs neurological development in children (Yehuda et al. 2006).
- Low iron in infancy affects behavioral and motor development (Corapci et al. 2006).

Thyroid Health, Depression, and Nutrients

Poor thyroid health is a common cause (or at least complication) of depression, particularly for women postpartum. If you have symptoms of hypothyroid (fatigue, unexplained weight gain, cold extremities), there is a simple test you can perform at home to begin to rule out thyroid problems. Monitor your first morning temperature: keep a thermometer on your night stand or under your pillow and take your temperature under your arm first thing in the morning, before rising. A temperature consistently under 97.5F indicates a low functioning thyroid. If you are still menstruating, days three through seven of your cycle will be the best days to test.

Your doctor can perform a test of your thyroid function. The general thyroid panels miss many diagnoses, so if your tests are negative and you still feel your thyroid is underactive, your doctor can measure T4, free T3, and reverse T3.

If your thyroid is confirmed to be low, you may be placed on a thyroid hormone. Ask for a natural form like Armour. But do not see hormone supplementation as a long-term solution. You may need more iodine. Your low iron may be interfering with your iodine metabolism. My thyroid function improved just by improving my vitamin and mineral levels. Yours can too, though it may be a long road.

CORRECTING MINERALS TAKES TIME

After World War II a study of magnesium-depleted patients found that it took more than a year to replenish the magnesium in their bodies (Seelig 1981). Frederickson (1989) reports that correcting a zinc deficiency in the brain takes at least three months. Raising blood levels of zinc through diet or supplementation will not cause a sudden change in brain levels.

Some parts of your body will be rebuilding longer than others and you need to supply those body parts with sufficient minerals over the long-term. Consider that a diet low in minerals and likely high in stress gave you this problem in the first place. Only a long-term change in your mineral intake will save you from lifelong problems with nutrient deficiencies.

RELIEF AND REBUILDING

Finding vitamins, minerals, and fats that you are deficient in, and then shoring those up, will alleviate your depression. You will not likely feel better overnight but you may get some relief in a few weeks' time. After some months you will probably find that your down cycles are shorter and less severe and come less often. Some people on antidepressant medication or therapies such as Saint John's Wort and amino acids are then able to work with their doctor to reduce their use of those methods.

But one nagging thing about nutrient deficiencies that we need to keep in mind is that they do not come out of a vacuum. If we are going to win the long-term battle against depression, we need to make some changes in our diet. We could avoid diet changes and rely on food supplements. That would be better than nothing. But food scientists have a knack for discovering new nutrients that no one knew about in the past. The nutrients were in our food all along (if our diets were good) but scientists did not know about them. The food supplement approach can help with the known nutrients, but not those that will eventually be discovered. Your best line of defense against depression still lies at the dinner table.

We know that most of us do not get the DRI of a lot of key depression-fighting nutrients. It is also the case that the DRI continues to be controversial. Many researchers and doctors believe the DRI for many nutrients is far too low. We should be consuming a whole lot more nutrients in our meals than the dinners that got us to this spot in the first place.

In fact, a researcher back in the 1930s collected food data on traditional societies across the globe and found diets of traditional societies were nutrient rich compared to the diets those people adopted as they became "civilized." Traditional diets contained five times the phosphorus and calcium and upwards of thirty times the magnesium and iron of modern diets (Price 2003).

Our long-term strategy needs to be making our food count. The first place to start is to look at what we eat and make it better. Everyday life offers us a host of choices and we just need to make them count. Some days we may even feel the "need" for a burger or macaroni and cheese. You can make those count too.

IMPROVING YOUR DIET

In the following food chapters you will find more information about food selection and food preparation than you probably ever wanted to know. Try not to become overwhelmed by it. Choose a food group chapter for a food you eat quite a bit and work on that one first. Little by little, you can make over your entire diet.

When your cooking starts to become a chore because you are obsessing about phytates in your food (you will understand what I mean when you read the grain and legume chapter), take a break and then work on another aspect of your diet.

My mom, who contributes relevant recipes to my Web site, observes that some of us more obsessive types can take the joy out of cooking very quickly with food preparation obsessions. That is not really the purpose here. The purpose is that we all become more aware of what we are eating and try to integrate some preparation techniques into our cooking that will add value to our food everyday. There are cheap and free ways to do just that.

As you begin to feel better with your added B vitamins, Omega-3 fatty acids, and whatever nutrients you have added to your diet or supplement regimen, spend some time on your food and make improvements. Put the food changes on a manageable timeline and visit my Web site to get some inspiration from my mom's creations.

Meats and Seafood

*Y*ou have to eat anyway. Make it count.

If you eat meat and seafood, this chapter is for you. You will learn to select your meats more wisely. Here's your cheat sheet before we begin:

Cheat Sheet

- Incorporate depression-busting meats into your diet.
- Beef is an excellent food source of iron and zinc and a good source of B vitamins. Its Omega-6 to Omega-3 ratio can be fairly healthy.
- Fish is an exceptional source of Omega-3 fatty acids.
- Select fish that have the most favorable Omega-3 to mercury ratio: wild salmon, sardines, anchovies, herring, and oyster.
- Eat wild-caught salmon and particularly chum, coho, and pink salmon.
- Add bone broth and organ meats to your diet.

The Skinny on Meats

I spent many years avoiding fats. On one weight-loss regimen in graduate school I lost about 15 pounds on a diet of less than 5 grams of fat a day. I ate pasta, vegetables, fruit, and some sort of imitation cheese wrapped in its own plastic wrapper. It is hard to eat plastic cheese for any length of time, but I maintained the view that a healthy diet was a low-fat vegetarian diet since that is what I was reading in all the popular health books.

As it turns out, our ancestors ate a good bit of meat—red, white, and whatever other meat colors were roaming in the forests and across the prairies. But the wild game that they ate was more lean in general, probably lower in saturated fat, and a bit higher in Omega-3 fatty acids and lower in Omega-6 fatty acids than the beef we buy in the grocery store.

Seafood and freshwater fish were also a popular choice of our ancestors. They are rich in vitamins, minerals, and in beneficial dietary fats. But with seafood as well, fish not allowed to live on their own native diets will not have the nutrient content of their counterparts living in the wild.

Unlike our ancestors, we have a plethora of meat choices available to us— it is simply a matter of selecting the best options from a very large menu. To help us focus on which foods will make our path to a depression-free life as short as possible, I have identified foods rich in our seven depression-fighting nutrients. I call these foods *depression busters*.

Depression Busters

The United States Department of Agriculture maintains an extensive data file on the nutritive value of more than 7,000 food items, including all the "depression nutrients" that foods contain. I examined the data to determine which foods contribute most to the Dietary Reference Intake (DRI) of our depression nutrients. A food high in B-6, B-12, folate, Omega-3 fatty acids, magnesium, and zinc would do well in this analysis. A food with an exceptional level of any one nutrient would do well also. Quite a few meat products, exotic and not so exotic, made it to the top of the list of depression busters.

At the top of our depression buster list are foods high in B-12. Beef liver, for instance, provides about one-half of the DRI of folate, vitamin B-6, and zinc. In addition, it provides more than twenty-nine times the DRI for vitamin B-12. Octopus fulfills the daily requirement for pregnant moms for DHA and EPA (Omega-3 fatty acids), more than half of the zinc and B-6 requirement, about one-third of the magnesium requirement, and more than twenty-five times the B-12 requirement.

Depression Busters

Meat	Game meat	Seafood and freshwater fish	
Emu	caribou	Clam	cisco
ostrich	whale	oyster	whitefish
lamb	seal	caviar, fish eggs	bluefish
beef	squirrel	herring	conch
tongue	rabbit	salmon*	sheefish
	opossum	mussel	spot
Organ meats	muskrat	trout	bass
liver	beaver	octopus	cuttlefish
kidney	raccoon	sablefish	wolffish
heart	moose	crab	halibut
spleen	elk	shad	smelt
pancreas	deer	sardine	spiny lobster
	bear	anchovy	pollack
		cod	sea trout
		tuna	drum
		whelk	
		*see page 105	

The depression buster meats will vindicate any hunter from days past: venison, bear, moose, squirrel, and rabbit have made the list. The depression buster meats will also vindicate any survivalist: raccoon, beaver, opossum, and muskrat are also included. Lovers of organ meats will be pleased as well: liver, kidney, heart, spleen, and pancreas have made the list. Brain would be on the list as well except that it can carry mad cow disease.

If you don't hunt or forage, do not worry. The meats that made the list tell us something very important: free-ranging animals in the wild are more nutritious than are their caged counterparts. Eat wild game if you have access, but another strategy is to eat the meat of animals raised on their native diet.

Meat Shopping Strategies

Best Choice: Don't Shop at All. Hunt and Trap Instead.

People who have known me for years are thinking "first she was depressed, but now *she really is crazy.*" We live on the edge of the Sequoia National

Forest and we have an abundance of food options as a result. I am starting to learn how to hunt, trap, and dress my own dinner. Hunting is cheaper than the market and the forest does not charge a gym membership.

The animals roaming in the forest are fairly lean, so they are a good option for someone still afraid to eat fat but wanting some beneficial fats in their diet. And, of course, if you hunt them yourself, you are working off all the calories in the process.

Best Gourmet Option: Pastured, Free-Range, Omega-Enriched

Animals allowed to graze on their natural diets of grass (in the case of cattle, sheep, and pigs) and grasses and bugs (in the case of fowl) tend to have a healthier meat profile. Even among ruminant animals with a four-chambered stomach (cattle and sheep), there is some evidence that a grass-based feeding system increases the Omega-3 fatty acids in their meat. Sheep allowed to graze on grass have an Omega-6 to Omega-3 ratio of about 1:1 while sheep fed primarily grain have a ratio of 7:1 (Demirel et al. 2006). The pork from free-ranging pigs has a more beneficial Omega-6 to Omega-3 fatty acid profile than the pork from pigs raised indoors (Muriel et al. 2002). The grass-fed meat market in this country sells to a higher-end customer. It tends to be organic as well or at least organic practices are used. This meat may be ideal for people who can afford it.

A meat marketing angle on the horizon is meat that is "Omega-3-enriched." Like the Omega-3 enriched eggs I discuss in the dairy and egg chapter, ranchers may begin to finish beef cattle, pigs, and poultry on diets that include flax seed, fish products, or marine-based algae. "Finishing" is the animal husbandry term used to describe primarily the feeding system used in the last weeks or months of the animal's life before slaughter. The flax or marine products contain Omega-3 fatty acids and the animal uptakes those beneficial fats in its finishing diet and deposits them into its own body fat. When that body fat hits your dinner plate, it will then help you with your depression, risk of heart disease, and risk of diabetes. Watch the marketplace for such innovations. The key phrase to look for is "flax-fed" or "Omega-enriched" (as it is in the case of the egg products). These foods have the potential to be depression buster meats. Following are some of the documented benefits:

- The depression-fighting Omega-3 fatty acid DHA increased four times in the thigh meat of chicken when the chicken's diet was supplemented with fish oil (Huang et al. 1990).
- In a study of pork, pigs fed a diet enriched with flaxseed for twenty days had a more favorable Omega-6 to Omega-3 ratio (about 3:1) than did those fed a regular diet (about 8:1) (Kouba et al. 2003)
- Flaxseed finishing of beef affects most the ALA content. The Omega-6 to Omega-3 ratio is improved from about 3.6 to 1 to 2.5 to 1 according to one study (Kronberg et al. 2006).
- In the flax feeding studies, the primary change in the muscle tends to be in the ALA content of the fat, not in the depression-fighting EPA or DHA. The Omega-6 to Omega-3 ratio is improved, but you can also get the added ALA from eating ground flaxseed directly.

Best Commercial Market Option: Beef and Lamb

Given that I spent much of my life eating plants with the occasional skinless chicken breast, I am sometimes struck by the irony illustrated in my freezer. At any given time, you will find quite an assortment of beef cattle parts in the freezer that make their way into soups and roasts in this house. We purchase an entire steer and use every part that the butcher can give us. Beef is a good food solution for us because it is raised 2 miles from our house on the edge of the Sequoia National Forest. It is also filled with depression-fighting nutrients.

Both beef and lamb make the depression buster list. The nutrient profiles that got them on the list are from the USDA, from the cuts available in your supermarket. These are not gourmet items. The beef and lamb is not labeled as grass-fed or organic.

But an interesting tidbit about the beef and lamb industries is that animal husbandry practices and market forces in the United States tend to work in our favor. It is generally cheaper for a cattle rancher to graze cattle in the mountains or on the prairie than to feed cattle a diet exclusively of grain.

I have seen many references on the Internet to cattle living their lives on feedlots. A drive through cattle country (or a look out my window) will give you a better idea of how cattle graze.

Beef cattle spend most of their lives grazing and are then finished on grain in feedlots for three to four months. It is their time in the feedlots that has captured the attention of animal rights activists. It is also during this feedlot time that they receive growth hormones to get them to market weight more quickly.

Grain versus Grass Finishing

For our purposes, the Omega-6 to Omega-3 ratio in the beef becomes less favorable during grain finishing. How much less favorable the ratio becomes is up for debate. One study found that it increases only from about 2:1 to 3:1 (Duckett et al. 1993). Studies of beef cattle spending their life on grain, like a show animal raised by a member of 4-H or Future Farmers of America, may have a ratio of about 10:1 compared to under 2:1 for a grass-fed animal (Enser et al. 1998).

What we have been able to do for our family is connect with a local rancher who will finish a steer to our specifications. We do not use growth hormones because we are not concerned about market weight and the steer has been given some grain depending on the local grass levels in the months before slaughter. Purists will purchase a steer finished on green grass and probably hang the carcass for one month before processing (as opposed to two weeks) to make the meat more tender.

If you want a freezer full of beef too and do not know how to get it, start asking around. There are small cattle ranches all over and the ranchers may be willing to finish the steer to your specifications. Expect to pay more for this service, but the bulk purchase will make up for any additional cost. We pay just under $3.50 per pound for the packaged beef (including cuts ranging from shanks to filet mignon).

Trim the Meat?

While the Omega-6 to Omega-3 ratio of beef muscle meat is favorable to our cause, the ratio in the adipose tissue is not. As you work to improve your ratio, you will want to trim your steaks. If you need a roast cooked in all of its fat like grandma used to make, that may be another matter entirely, but it will not really help the Omega-6 to Omega-3 cause.

Freshwater Fish and Seafood

Some societies have lived primarily on wild-caught fish. Increasingly such a diet is less healthy because of the levels of toxins in the oceans, lakes, and rivers and, thus, in our fish supply. The whole fish-shopping experience has become complex based on three issues:

(1) **Mercury**

The Environmental Protection Agency asks us to eat no more than two fish meals per week (up to 12 ounces per week) of low mercury content fish. Our depression buster list is filled with seafood that we should only eat in measured quantities. In the inset article on the next page I provide the top five depression buster seafood items that have the best ratio of Omega-3 fatty acids to mercury. Those are your best bets for regular consumption.

(2) **How the fish were raised—in the wild or farmed**

How fish were raised affects their fat content. Wild fish tend to have very low levels of Omega-6 fatty acids and high levels of Omega-3 fatty acids. Farmed salmon actually has a higher content of Omega-3 fatty acids than wild fish since farms have moved toward feeding fish food high in Omega-3 fatty acids. But the Omega-6 to Omega-3 ratio is still less favorable than the wild-caught variety. Furthermore, the feed provided in farms tends to have more toxins in it than the food fish eat in the wild. Wild-caught fish will be lower in toxins and will have a more favorable Omega-6 to Omega-3 ratio.

(3) **Where the fish live**

Some oceans are more polluted than others. Fish caught in one part of the world may have a lower level of toxins than fish caught in another part of the world. Thus, there is variation in toxins across fish breeds depending on their location and there is variation across fish species as well. To find out what is safe in your area, visit the Web site of the Monterey Bay Aquarium. This site provides a list of fish available in each region of the country, which are grown or harvested in a sustainable fashion: http://www.mbayaq.org/cr/seafoodwatch.asp.

The Ocean's Alive Web site provides lists of fish and environmental pollutants: http://www.oceansalive.org.

Salmon Risk

Salmon has topped our list of foods with the most favorable Omega-3 to mercury ratio. In fact, in many samples of salmon collected by the EPA, no mercury has been detected. Salmon's high fatty acid content, of course, is

---

Mercury, Fish, and Seafood

Three fish made the depression-buster list based on nutrients but I excluded them because of their high mercury content. The Environmental Protection Agency warns us not to eat shark, king mackerel, and tilefish. Don't eat them. Some species of mackerel and tilefish are safe and if you have access, you can consider them to be depression busters.

Of the remaining depression-busting fish and seafood, I was able to obtain the Omega-3 content and mercury content for all seafood except the most obscure. Of our depression busters, I list here the top five with the most favorable ratio of Omega-3 fatty acids to mercury. For your seafood meals, start with these choices.

- wild salmon
- sardines
- anchovies
- herring
- oyster

therapeutic for depression. But not all salmon fillets are created equal and the story of fish and pollution does not stop at mercury. Other environmental pollutants and possible health hazards such as PCBs and dioxins are in fish as well (and in all other foods to some degree).

In a 2005 study reported in the *Journal of Nutrition*, researchers collected salmon samples from across the globe and examined their fatty acid profile and their level of toxins. They performed a risk analysis associated with eating fish and estimate that if we consumed wild salmon with an equivalent of 1 gram of EPA plus DHA each day, our cancer risk would be eight times the acceptable level (based on a range of risk provided by the Environmental Protection Agency). With farmed salmon, our risk would be twenty-four times the acceptable level for cancer risk. Both provide good sources of Omega-3 fatty acids. But both have levels of toxins that do not allow us to eat them every day, according to this research (Foran et al. 2005).

When you eat salmon, reduce your risk by selecting more favorable varieties of wild salmon (Foran et al. 2005) such as chum, coho, and pink.

Cod Liver Oil and Fish Oil

Because of the pollutants in fish, it is wise to reduce your fish consumption, particularly if you are pregnant, breastfeeding, or having health problems related to heavy metals. But an alternative to eating fish is consuming cod liver oil or fish oil. The cod liver oil and fish oil products in this country are molecularly distilled to filter out the contaminants. You get the oils without the pollution.

A fish oil supplement is a great solution to increasing your Omega-3 intake in the short-term. As I mentioned in the section on Omega-3 fatty acids and depression, Andrew Stoll recommends 4 grams of EPA a day for depression. It would be practically impossible to consume that much EPA in a day in your food. A salmon fillet of 100 grams (3.5 ounces) will provide you with about 1 gram of EPA and 1 gram of DHA, both depression-fighting Omega-3 fatty acids. Since it is not recommended that we eat salmon for every meal, everyday, an oil supplement may be in order. If you take a supplement, you can improve the Omega-6 to Omega-3 ratio in your diet at the same time. Over the longer term, you will find the supplement to be less necessary.

The difference between fish oil and cod liver oil is that the fish oil is made from the muscle meat of the fish and the cod liver oil is made from the liver of the cod. Cod liver oil naturally provides a good supply of vitamin A and vitamin D, which makes it my preferred choice. If you use cod liver oil and are taking the high therapeutic doses recommended in depression research, you will want to be sure to buy a brand with lower vitamin levels lest you end up consuming too much vitamin A and D. You can also take a combination of cod liver oil and fish oil to obtain your therapeutic level of Omega-3s without too much vitamin A or D. I provide up-to-date information on my Web site.

THE REST OF THE ANIMAL

Organ Meats

I was not surprised that so many organ meats made it to our list of depression busters. Traditional diets across the globe have contained organ meat in the form of liver, heart, brain, and kidney. My grandma and grandpa used to keep "hog head cheese" in their refrigerator, a staple in their diet that they used on sandwiches. The grandkids said "eewwww" and ate bologna instead, a meat that more cleverly hid all the animal parts used in its production.

Liver is much maligned because of the liver's function of processing toxins. Heavy metals and other toxins travel through the liver before they are excreted through the bowels. But it is that toxin pathway that creates a meat full of nutrients. The fact is that the body needs vitamins and minerals to break down those toxins and eliminate them. Those vitamins and minerals, including the B vitamin family and zinc, are housed in the liver. Liver is a highly nutritious meat but it does have a higher level of toxins than the muscle meat of an animal (Lopez-Alonso et al. 2000). To reduce the level of toxins in liver, buy organic calf liver. It is a rich and inexpensive source of nutrition.

Sautéed Liver and Onions

Around here, we soak the liver in lemon juice, sauté chopped onions until they have a nice caramelized glaze, set the onions aside, and cook the liver (which has been coated in a flour, salt, and pepper mix). When the liver is done, we make gravy and top the liver with the onions and gravy. It is really not that bad. I cannot say that it is particularly good, but it does increase my energy level. Some bacon fat will take the liver to another level, approaching not-so-bad in my opinion. Serve with cooked greens and quartered, garden-ripe tomatoes.

Organic liver is fairly easy to find, usually at any health food store that carries meat. I have seen sweetbreads and heart regularly at Whole Foods as well. You will not likely find beef brain anywhere because of the possibility of the meat carrying mad cow disease.

Bones

As a nation, we worry about getting enough minerals into our bones to prevent osteoporosis, but we don't tend to incorporate animal bone into our diet, a rich source of minerals for our own bones and a relatively inexpensive source. We know that the magnesium in our own bodies is found mostly in our bones. Animal bones provide a great source of calcium and magnesium as well as a host of other minerals. Eating bone broths is an easy way to incorporate these minerals into our diets. On my Web site, you will find many soups made with a simple bone broth, courtesy of my mother.

To-Do List: Meat and Seafood

- Incorporate depression-busting meats into your diet.
- Investigate sources of pastured beef and lamb if you eat these meats; incorporate these pastured sources into your diet.

Make One Change with Broth

Make one pot full of broth each week. Put soup bones in your stock pot or slow cooker with one-quarter cup of high-quality apple cider vinegar. Cook on low for about twelve hours. Strain out the bones and use them for one more batch if you wish. It will not be as rich and flavorful, but it will have additional minerals that did not get drawn out of the bones during the first round.

If you have no time to make soup with the broth or to use it as a base in a sauté, warm up a bowl's worth of broth and eat it. I often eat mine for breakfast. Salt to taste and you are good to go.

Preferably start with organic bones from grass-fed beef. I find organic bones at Whole Foods for $2/pound. A $4 package could keep me in soup stock for a week. You might be able to find some bones on the cheap at a traditional butcher shop.

- Select fish that have the most favorable Omega-3 to mercury ratio.
- Eat wild-caught salmon and particularly chum, coho, and pink salmon.
- Add bone broth and organ meats to your diet.

∽ 10 ~

Dairy and Eggs

We are a family of egg lovers and eggs can be a great source of depression-busting Omega-3 fatty acids. We are such fans of eggs that we recently raised twenty chicks in one of our porch rooms in anticipation of a springtime bounty. That experiment became an indoor air disaster, but the chicks are still around and living in proper quarters. If you eat a lot of eggs or dairy, make them count. Read on for more detail but here is your cheat sheet to start:

Cheat Sheet

- Investigate sources of free-range eggs at farmers' markets or buy some "designer" Omega-3 eggs at the supermarket; incorporate them into your diet.
- Replace your regular dairy products with dairy from grass-fed animals to add Omega-3 fatty acids to your diet.
- Culture that milk to add B vitamins to your diet.

Dairy and egg products have been popular food items in the American diet but both groups faced a decline in the last part of the twentieth century and are only recently making a comeback.

According to consumption rates maintained by the USDA, egg consumption peaked in 1945 at 410 eggs per person per year. People apparently spent their butter and sugar money on eggs during the war since eggs were not rationed.

Consumption dropped again after the war and began a steady decline to 239 eggs per person per year in 1998. In the 1990s, eggs began to come back into fashion with the introduction of "designer" eggs rich in Omega-3 fatty acids.

Milk consumption has declined from about 34 gallons per person per year in the early 1900s to about 22 gallons in the early 2000s. However, there is a small but growing demand for raw milk from grass-fed cows, milk that is not pasteurized or homogenized as is most milk sold in this country.

The egg renaissance in particular is important for depression because the designer eggs add value to our foods in the form of depression-busting nutrients. These designer eggs are available commercially and a good asset to your diet if you eat eggs. However, the gold standard (and official depression buster) is the egg from a hen allowed to range on weeds and bugs.

DEPRESSION-BUSTER EGGS

In the USDA nutrient database, from which I determined the list of depression busters, there are no conventional foods that make the list. Goose eggs and duck eggs are depression busters, but you are not likely to find them at the supermarket. They are also higher in cholesterol than regular eggs, which may not be recommended by your doctor if you do not metabolize cholesterol properly.

However, based on studies of free-range eggs and their added fat content, we can add the free-range chicken egg to the list as well. Its additional Omega-3 content plus the vitamin and mineral profile provided by the USDA push the egg into the depression-busting category (see Simopoulos and Salem 1989 for data). Keep in mind, however, that it is the yolk of the egg that puts the egg into this depression-busting category. Egg whites alone would not make the list.

Depression Busters

free-range goose egg	free-range chicken egg
free-range duck egg	

As with meats, our egg-based depression busters lend evidence to an important point: how the animal is raised affects the nutrients it provides us. The conventional supermarket egg does not make the list, but the free-range egg does.

Because of the relatively low value of depression nutrients in dairy and eggs as a class, we need to do some work shopping for the best quality dairy and eggs and we can even do some food preparation to improve their depression-fighting qualities.

Shopping: Pastured and Organic

Cows, goats, and chickens were intended to graze freely. Cows eat grasses, chickens eat grasses and small insects, and goats eat just about anything not tacked down. When these animals are eating a traditional diet, their milk and eggs are higher in the beneficial Omega-3 fatty acids and lower in Omega-6 fatty acids.

Free-Range Eggs

Like the difference between the muscle meat of cattle allowed to graze freely on grass and those that are not, chickens allowed to range freely, eating grass and bugs, produce eggs that are a vastly different than the standard eggs you will find in the supermarket.

If our goal is to get our diet as close to the recommended ratio of Omega-6 to Omega-3 fatty acids daily of 1:1, a free-range chicken egg actually puts us well into that ratio, whereas a supermarket egg will jeopardize our diets. In a study of the difference between supermarket eggs and eggs of free-ranging Greek hens, researchers found that the ratio of Omega-6 to Omega-3 in the common supermarket egg was nearly 20:1 compared to a ratio of approximately 1:1 for free range-eggs (Simopoulus and Salem 1989). The free-range Greek egg had lower levels of Omega-6 fatty acids and higher levels of Omega-3 fatty acids than the supermarket eggs, a depression-busting combination.

The Greek hens were grazing on a plant called purslane, rich in Omega-3 fatty acids. During the winter in dry years, my hens graze on almost nothing fresh, so their eggs would not be as healthy as the Greek egg even though they are free-range. If you are selecting free-range eggs at a farmers' market, just ask the farmer about the hens' access to grasses and weeds. When you get the eggs home, a darker yolk is an indication that the hen is eating bugs and weeds with beneficial nutrients.

Omega-3 Enriched Eggs

The potential of eggs for health has not gone unnoticed in the marketplace. Nearly every supermarket these days has a selection of "designer eggs," rich in Omega-3s. These designer eggs are, in fact, higher in Omega-3s, but not because of a free-range diet. The hens receive a diet that contains flaxseed, a vegetarian source of Omega-3s. A hen diet of 20 percent flax might get the ratio of Omega-6 to Omega-3 as low as 1.4:1 (Zhang and Watson 2002).

If you do not have access to free-range eggs, which are sometimes available at farmers' markets, shop for designer eggs but make sure the label mentions "Omega-3 enriched" or "flax-fed" to ensure that you are getting your money's worth. This is a very simple way to add the Omega-3 fatty acids DHA and EPA to your diet if your diet includes eggs.

Make One Change with Eggs

One 1996 study in *Nutrition* found that in nursing mothers, the addition of two "designer eggs" a day to their diet for a six-week period changed the ratio of the Omega-6 to Omega-3 fatty acids in their breast milk from about 7:1 to 3:1 (Cherian and Sim 1996). Just two eggs a day enriched the breast milk of these moms.

Milk from Grazing Cows

A theme in this book is that, much like our own diets affect our health, the diets of the animals we eat affects their meat and egg quality. So too may diets affect milk quality. Studies of cows' milk find that cows on diets of fresh green grass have a higher content of beneficial fatty acids than those on diets of hay and grain (Bargo et al. 2006; Schroeder et al. 2005; Dhiman et al. 1999; Hebeisen 1994; Couvreur et al. 2006). However, we can make too much of this finding. Milk is not the path to a high intake of Omega-3 fatty acids.

However, if you drink milk and eat butter, finding a source that allows the cows to graze may help you increase the level of Omega-3 fatty acids in your diet and reduce your intake of Omega-6. The dairy products will also be higher in other fat soluble vitamins and beneficial fats.

Preparation: Raw and Cultured

Egg Cooking

Eggs can be one of your primary strategies for increasing Omega-3 fatty acids and protein in your diet. The egg white is rich in protein and the egg yolk is potentially a rich source of Omega-3s. About two-thirds of the egg white is protein and the pattern of amino acids in the egg white matches nearly perfectly the requirement for protein in the human diet. When you find amino acid blends in the supplement section of your health food store, many of them will have the amino acid profile of an egg, considered the protein gold standard. Unlike most other foods, egg whites should be cooked. The heat increases the digestibility of the protein (Bolourchi-Veghefi 2002).

As with other foods, cooking will reduce the vitamin content of eggs. In a 2002 study, Bedogni and Battistini compared the effect of cooking on the vitamin content of an egg. They found that a fried egg had 20 percent less folic acid and 36 percent less B-12 than a raw egg.

So it is ideal for egg whites to be cooked to improve the digestibility of the egg protein, even though some vitamins will be lost. Egg yolks will retain more vitamins if they are raw. My husband eats his eggs sunny side up, with the yolks remaining slightly runny—this is a good solution to the problem.

Culture the Milk

Milk by itself does not contain an abundance of depression-fighting nutrients, but when it is cultured, you are adding value to your milk product.

Yogurt

Yogurt is milk that has been cultured—it has been heated, cooled, a bacteria strain added, and allowed to sit in a warm environment. The final product ends up slightly soured, more solid, and filled with beneficial bacteria. As the bacteria works on your milk to make yogurt, the bacteria also produce B vitamins. In a review article by Shahani and Chandan they provide data on the added levels of folic acid and B-12 in cultured products. They find that with an incubation time of sixteen hours:

- the amount of B-12 in yogurt increases about four-fold (though it may not all be useable by your body as B-12)
- the folic acid content increases fourteen-fold

Yogurt you find in the store is likely not cultured for sixteen hours so you cannot expect a fourteen-fold increase in folic acid in your store-bought yogurt. A good vitamin-maximizing strategy is to culture your own yogurt for sixteen hours or longer.

In the Appendix, I include instructions for making yogurt, including warnings about not heating it too much in the process. The heat will reduce the folate that you are trying to increase.

Kefir

Another approach to culturing milk is to make kefir (KEH-fear), a process most people find to be easier than yogurt. To culture kefir you need kefir grains. The grains look nothing like a wheat kernel. They actually look a whole lot more like cauliflower, but they are a symbiotic mass of bacteria and yeasts that act like a yogurt or sourdough starter. You simply add milk to the grains, wait a day, strain out the grains, and you have a refreshing drink filled with beneficial bacteria, B vitamins, and enzymes.

The grains multiply as well, so all you need to do to start making kefir is to find someone with grains. I have actually shipped grains to people all over the country until our postmaster put a stop to it.

"It is perfectly legal to send by mail these little cauliflower-looking things in plastic baggies, soaked in milk, all wrapped in a washcloth," I said.

I even wrote a letter to include with each package (included below), but to no avail. Increasingly, though, the postmaster is softening and the shipping has begun again.

My mom, who loves plain yogurt, loves to drink kefir plain. The rest of us dress it up a bit. We add fruit and honey and mix it up in a blender like a milk shake. Our son, Frederick, loves it.

Dairy culture resources
- Sandor Katz, *Wild Fermentation*
- Dom's "Kefir in-site": http://users.chariot.net.au/~dna/kefirpage.html

Milk and Iron

Milk and dairy products as a group make the point that it is important to investigate what nutrients you may be deficient in before your create your meal plan. There is evidence, for instance, that consuming dairy products with a meal will reduce your absorption of iron. If you are iron deficient, you are probably best served by avoiding dairy products with your meals.

Dear Postmaster,

Enclosed are kefir grains, a starter for making a fermented milk drink, like yogurt. I put about a tablespoon of milk in the baggie to keep the kefir grains alive during transit. If you are reading this note it is likely because my foolproof double baggie and washcloth packing method was not entirely foolproof. I apologize for that.

Just to let you know, this combination of milk and weird stuff freaked out our postmaster, Dean. Dean is a lover of controversy and he is a great story teller, but I don't think he wants any excitement surrounding the little California Hot Springs post office. Folks have a long memory here and some misunderstanding about my little priority mail package would linger long in the minds of the locals. It would probably be catalogued with the time one of the local water districts got a new water tank and brought it in by helicopter. Or perhaps it would be remembered along with the time the large boulder fell onto the road and we all showed up with our picnic lunches to watch it get blasted into pieces. The excitement might even be compared to the small forest fire we had up here this summer. Dean, as part of the emergency response team, evacuated our little road.

But I digress. These are kefir grains, a bacteria culture that ferments dairy products. Sourdough bread, yogurt, and that Amish friendship bread that was a big hit in my college dorm all need some sort of starter just like these kefir grains. So what I am trying to say is that these kefir grains are not part of some terrorist plot from California Hot Springs, nor a militia plot. They are not even related to the recent marijuana busts in California Hot Springs (which Dean could tell you a great deal about). Indeed, they are just about making folks healthy. These grains help turn regular old milk into a "power drink" filled with beneficial bacteria, vitamins, and enzymes. The bacteria colonize your intestinal tract and help build a healthy immune system. To prove to Dean that these kefir grains are not weapons of any sort, I brought some to the post office to eat in front of him and have offered him some to taste as well. Yes, you can eat the grains, but don't eat them all because then you will have nothing to drink. Here's some more information:

http://users.chariot.net.au/~dna/kefirpage.html

So, please contact me if you would like some, but please forward these grains on to the recipient who is eagerly awaiting their arrival. Thank you very much.

Sincerely,

Amanda Rose

The Raw Milk Debate

Pasteurization of milk is a fairly new phenomenon in the history of food. Pasteurization heats the milk to kill most of the pathogenic bacteria and, of course, the beneficial bacteria at the same time. Small farmers with their own cows or goats typically consume milk raw from their own animals even today. There is also a small but growing market for raw milk commercially. We can buy raw milk in California and I often do, but my own choice is highly controversial. In fact, it is illegal to sell raw milk in many states in the United States.

From a depression-fighting point of view, raw milk does contain more B vitamins than its pasteurized counterpart but not enough to make raw milk a depression-buster food. The added B vitamin content will not be of value to you either if the potential for contamination would concern you. Worry alone will separate you from some of those B vitamins. You can read more about milk research and this food politics issue on my Web site.

To-Do List: Dairy and Eggs

- Investigate sources of free-range eggs at farmers' markets or buy some "designer" Omega-3 eggs at the supermarket; incorporate them into your diet.
- Replace your regular dairy products with dairy from grass-fed animals to add Omega-3 fatty acids to your diet.
- Culture your milk to add B vitamins to your diet.

Fruits and Vegetables

here is a mind-boggling amount of conflicting dietary advice in the world today but there is almost universal acceptance that we need more fresh produce in our diets, especially vegetables. If you do not eat a lot of produce, read this chapter anyway because on good days you should work on adding more produce to your diet. Here's your cheat sheet to pack a punch in your diet with produce:

Cheat Sheet

- Eat fruits and vegetables that are as fresh as possible and ripe (but not overripe) to maximize the vitamin content of your diet.
- Select heirloom varieties.
- Eat local produce.
- Ferment fruits and vegetables to improve the B vitamin content of your diet and to increase your intake of beneficial bacteria.
- To maximize the minerals you are digesting, reduce the oxalic acid in your diet by avoiding or boiling, steaming, or fermenting vegetables high in oxalates.

Fruits and vegetables provide fiber to our diets. In their raw form, they add digestive enzymes to our stomachs. They can be good sources of cancer-fighting antioxidants. Vegetables are low in calories and will offset some of the higher calorie depression buster foods. Fresh produce provides good dietary sources of magnesium and folate, important depression nutrients. We should eat fresh produce often, particularly raw, with all nutrients intact.

But there is only one fruit or vegetable in the USDA database that has the nutrient-dense properties of our other depression busters: the red chili pepper.

Depression Buster
red chili pepper

Part of the problem is that fruits and vegetables, like milk, contain a lot of water—100 grams of broccoli contains more water than 100 grams of beef liver. My analysis of depression busters is by weight and, thus, broccoli is at a bit of a disadvantage. However, even dried tomatoes and carrot chips did not make the cut with their water removed. Nutritional yeast, algae (spirulina), kelp, and an assortment of herbs and spices technically made the cut but 100 grams of each of these is about 6 cups. That seems like a lot of spirulina. And for that matter, 100 grams of garlic made the cut but few people are going to eat thirty-three cloves of garlic.

And so I apologize to the world of fruit and vegetables for making a list with only one lone rebel, red hot chili peppers. Thank you to the men in my family who proved to me that it is possible for humans to eat 100 grams of hot peppers in a sitting.

But back to the rest of the produce world. There may be some important reasons that no other fruit or vegetable in the USDA database made the list. The foods in the database may have been transported over long distances before they were tested. They are probably the newer hybrid varieties that tend to be less nutrient-rich than are the heirloom crops that were prevalent many years ago.

Vegetables Yesterday and Today

Vegetables in the USDA database are at a severe disadvantage today in making the depression buster cut than they would have been fifty years ago. The USDA has collected data on the nutrient values of food for over a century and in 1950 published a comprehensive list of nutrient values for food. Those

1950 nutrient values are fascinating: nutrient values were much greater in 1950 than they are today.

Researchers analyzed systematically forty-three garden crop foods and found a decline in nutrient values for protein, calcium, phosphorus, iron, riboflavin, and ascorbic acid. Food in 1999 had about 85 percent of the iron content of food in 1950 (Davis et al. 2004). Data on our other depression-fighting minerals—magnesium and zinc—are not available over that time period.

However, in 1963 the USDA did publish magnesium values for some foods and among the top magnesium foods today listed in the USDA database, comparable data for spinach and beet greens are available. After adjusting for differences in their water content, spinach today has only about 75 percent of the magnesium that spinach samples had in 1963. Beet greens today have about 70 percent of the magnesium of yesteryear.

What we do not know from this food nutrient data is the key question—why has there been a decline in nutrient values? One argument is that the mineral levels in our soil have been compromised. On the other hand, Davis and colleagues argue that the cause is likely due to changes in plant varieties rather than in soil depletion. Many nutrient values have declined, including potassium even though potassium is added to crops with conventional fertilizer. So with potassium values on the decline, a more likely suspect is the change in plant varieties themselves.

New hybrid plants are developed to maximize crop yield and to transport and store well. When plants are selectively bred for one characteristic, other beneficial characteristics of the original plant are likely to decline in the new hybrid. A high nutrient content is typically sacrificed when plants are bred to produce more food or to stay fresh in cold storage.

As a society, when we buy produce from large grocers, we are, in fact, paying for lesser-quality food. And it is that behavior that we can change to help us in our depression fight. There are no depression busters on the fruit and vegetable list, but perhaps there could be. Produce grown in my little orchard might make the cut.

In general, how food is grown matters for its nutrient content. How it is transported matters. How we prepare it matters. If we make wise selections, we will improve the nutrient content of our diet. We might even find a depression buster or two in our own backyard garden or at a farmers' market. In fact, if you have access to a lab and think you have found a depression buster, please contact me.

Buy Organic, Local, and Heirloom Produce

You will maximize the vitamin and mineral content in your vegetables and fruits if you can buy organic, local, and heirloom varieties.

Organic Produce May Be Richer in Minerals

If part of the reason for the historic decline in nutrients in American and British produce is soil depletion due to the use of synthetic fertilizers, one solution is to buy organic produce. Buying organic will add minerals to your body and because of the lower levels of chemical residues on the produce, you will reduce your body's need for nutrients as well.

Organic farmers are more likely to be using composting methods that return all nutrients to the soil, not just those nutrients found in synthetic fertilizers. As a result, organic produce may be likely to have higher mineral content.

To inspire us to buy organic, a 1993 study published in the *Journal of Applied Nutrition* describes results conducted at Doctor's Data Laboratory in Chicago on five fruits and vegetables. Researchers shopped at Chicago-area markets over a two year period and collected samples of fruits, vegetables, and wheat, some of which were organic and some of which were not organic. They tested the mineral content of each. Organic corn, for instance, contained four times the magnesium, nearly three times the zinc, and about two and one-half times the iron (Smith 1993).

Organic foods are expensive. Most of us cannot afford a 100 percent organic diet. The Environmental Working Group, an online advocacy group, has developed The Dirty Dozen, a list of the foods most likely to have pesticide residue—foods that you should buy organic or avoid.

The Dirty Dozen

1. peaches
2. strawberries
3. apples
4. spinach
5. nectarines
6. celery
7. pears
8. cherries
9. potatoes
10. sweet bell peppers
11. raspberries
12. imported grapes

For more information, visit the Environmental Working Group online: http://www.ewg.org

Alcohol and Depression

Alcohol is not only a depressive drug, but it actually depletes your body of depression-fighting nutrients. B vitamins in particular are lost as you drink. Studies in humans of blood levels of folate show that hours after a drink, our blood levels of folate fall (Stowell 2000). Folate is difficult enough to get in our diets, it seems like a good idea to take it easy on the drinks.

Heirloom Varieties

Heirloom varieties tend to be higher in nutrients than newer hybrid varieties of produce you find in the grocery store. Produce varieties are being developed for use in commercial agriculture with a mind toward yield, transportation, and pest control. They excel in producing an abundant crop, in traveling well, and in being resistant to pests. They also appear to be decreasingly nutritious.

Molasses is Magnesium Heaven

The white sugar we add to our coffee and tea is made from sugar cane. As it is refined, 99 percent of the magnesium is lost (Marier 1986). The "waste" product of that refining process, molasses, is rich in magnesium.

Heirloom varieties are not going to be grown by larger farms because they pose transportation and storage problems. They tend to be grown by small organic farmers who will pick them right before market and take them to the farmers' market or local health food store. Those organic farmers use methods that add a variety of nutrients back to the soil, not just NPK—nitrogen (N), phosphorus (P), and potassium (K). The heirloom plants are likely to be grown in richer soil and they are likely to take up more nutrients through their roots than would a newer hybrid variety.

The use of hybrids may be the single largest contributor to the decline of nutrients in our produce since the 1950s. Not only should we eat wild game like our ancestors, we should use the seeds they used in their gardens. If you garden, you can find catalogues of heirloom seeds and the catalogue will describe their characteristics. You will find some produce notable for its nutrient content.

Local Produce May Have a Higher Nutrient Content

Produce that is not local, by definition, must be transported. That transportation time is storage time. Fresh vegetables that are stored lose vitamin content. Among our depression nutrients, folate is the most likely nutrient to be affected by transport and storage. Folate is heat-sensitive and the level of folate in our fruits and vegetables is most likely to decline if the food is not stored in cold storage or in a refrigerator.

Many small farmers who sell their produce at farmers' markets will pick their crops the evening and morning before the market. This is very fresh produce. Some vendors bring produce from other farms, depending on the rules of the market. You want to find the freshest produce at your market, so look for the smaller vendors and ask when they harvest.

Otherwise, it is actually the larger operations that will be able to preserve the produce and its nutrient value. Large cold storage facilities do this well but what they are storing is likely to be a hybrid variety.

Store your own purchases in the refrigerator.

BEST FRESH AND RIPE

Frozen and canned fruits and vegetables are not devoid of nutrition, but they have lost a considerable amount in their processing. One of our key depression-related vitamins is B-6 and B-6 is lost pretty quickly through freezing and canning. The loss of B-6 through canning ranges from about 20 percent to 75 percent in the studies cited below. Keep in mind that as the can sits on the shelf, time will also erode that vitamin B-6 further. The freezer is a good preservation method, but you will have vitamin loss in frozen goods as well. Losses of B-6 content range from 10 percent in tomatoes to 33 percent in summer squash.

To the degree that you can incorporate fresh foods into your diet, you will improve your vitamin and mineral intake. I know it is not always possible, but keep in mind these differences as you prepare foods.

Table 11.1: Canned foods and vitamin B-6 loss	
	% loss of B-6
Cabbage	19[a]
Cherries	20[b]
Green beans	45[b]
Lima beans	53[a]
Spinach	75[a]

a Schroeder 1971
b Abou-Fadel and Miller 1983

Table 11.2: Frozen foods and vitamin B-6 loss	
	% loss of B-6
Tomatoes	10
Fruit and Juices 12 varieties, average	15
Broccoli	23
Spinach	32
Summer squash	33
Source: Schroeder 1971	

The vitamin content of fruits and vegetables tends to peak when the produce is ripe and then it begins to decline again. So if you have control over when your produce is picked, as home gardeners do, pick the produce when it is ripe (but not overripe) and use it as soon as possible. A vine-ripened tomato, warmed by the sun and carried to the table, is an epicurean delight. Simply slice, salt, and add dashes of oil and vinegar.

While fresh and ripe is a good general principle, some nutrients like folate and vitamin C are so susceptible to loss from storage and temperature that frozen might actually be better than a fresh item you have stored in your refrigerator.

Ferment Them

In my quest for optimum digestive help I found a great book by Sandor Katz called *Wild Fermentation* that convinced me to branch out into the fermented vegetable world. Fermentation adds B vitamins to our foods—we saw that with cultured milk. For added vitamin content, to preserve the vitamins in the raw produce, and to add beneficial bacteria to your diet, consider culturing vegetables. The bacteria will aid in your digestion, which will further promote your absorption of vitamins and minerals.

Fermentation takes some monitoring, but is really rather easy. I highly recommend it as a depression-busting nutritional strategy and I provide some basic instructions in the Appendix.

Fermented Kefir Sodas

There has never been an easier, more pleasant, and more inexpensive way to add magnesium to your diet: start making your own kefir sodas.

Kefir sodas made with water kefir grains are fruity, fizzy, and loaded with beneficial bacteria and enzymes. Yours can also be loaded with magnesium if you use unrefined raw cane sugar in your brew.

With each quart of water, you generally add one-third of a cup of sugar. If you use sucanat, your quart of soda will have about 40 milligrams of magnesium from the sugar alone—over 10 percent of the DRI. It is difficult to get a lot of magnesium from any one food source, so added fermented sodas will help in your dietary levels of magnesium. In that drink you will also get beneficial bacteria and enzymes. People pay a lot of money for probiotics and enzymes. Kefir is nature's way of saving your money.

See the Appendix for instructions or visit my Web site.

VEGETABLE SELECTION AND PREPARATION: OXALIC ACID LEVELS

Some vegetables are noted for their high content of oxalic acid that binds with minerals in your digestive tract and keeps the minerals from being absorbed. Oxalic acid is also the primary component of kidney stones. These are good reasons to reduce oxalic acid in your diet.

In an interesting study reported in the *British Journal of Nutrition* in 2004, researchers compared magnesium absorption from high-oxalate and low-oxalate food: spinach and kale. Participants were given a meal of phytate-free white bread and either spinach or kale, cooked and puréed. In the high oxalate spinach meal, study participants absorbed about 27 percent of the magnesium in the meal. In the low oxalate kale meal, participants absorbed about 37 percent of the magnesium. As with the phytate studies I describe in the next chapter, this study shows that you can increase your mineral absorption by eating foods lower in oxalic acid. (Bohn et al. 2004)

Reducing Oxalic Acid: Boil, Steam, or Ferment

A 2005 study found that boiling reduced the level of oxalic acid in food. Note in the table below that boiling spinach reduces oxalic acid by 87 percent whereas steaming reduces it by 42 percent. In every vegetable studied, boiling is more effective than steaming. And there is a good reason: unlike phytates where the phytase enzyme breaks down the phytic acid, as you will read about in the next chapter, oxalic acid is not "broken down" by cooking. It simply falls off of the food and into the water. You can then remove the oxalic acid by pitching the cooking water. So, the cooking strategy here is to boil (or at least steam) the food and discard the cooking water. I know that all our mothers saved this liquid for soup or gravy, but you'll want to toss the water of heavy offenders.

A more effective strategy is to ferment foods high in oxalates. This is my favorite strategy of course because you maintain the enzymes in the raw food, add beneficial bacteria to your diet, and increase the B vitamin content as I describe above. Boiling or steaming will also cause some mineral loss in the food.

Table 11.3: Oxalic acid content after cooking		
	Boiling, % reduced	Steaming, % reduced
Spinach	87	42
Green Swiss chard leaves	84	46
Broccoli	57	19
Carrots	56	53
Beet roots	31	6
Source: Chai and Liebman 2005		
Vegetables were chopped and cooked for 12 minutes.		

In a 2005 study in *Food Microbiology*, researchers found that the soluble iron in the homemade vegetable juice in the study increased sixteen times with fermentation. What this means is that if you juice your own vegetable juice with a high iron vegetable like spinach and you ferment it, your body may absorb *sixteen times* more iron than it would have absorbed had you consumed the juice right out of the juicer (Bergqvist et al. 2005).

The same study found that fermenting commercial juice increased the solubility of iron by seven times. So you can also buy a ready-to-drink juice and ferment it and digest about seven times the iron in the original juice.

The basic vegetable fermentation technique I describe in the Appendix will work for any of these foods. The water kefir process I describe will also be effective in fermenting vegetable juice.

What's High in Oxalic Acid

The oxalic acid big list below—the foods highest in oxalate—are the foods you would be better off avoiding if you have a choice. The big list includes foods you should avoid eating raw in large quantities. Beets are a popular choice in homemade raw vegetable juice, yet are high in oxalic acid. Carrots, parsley, and spinach tend to be eaten raw as well. Do not eat them in their raw form in great quantities; consider boiling them and tossing out the boiling water as an alternative to sautéing. Boiled vegetables can then be browned in oil if you do not like the taste of boiled produce.

The amount of oxalic acid in food samples is highly variable and, thus, so are oxalic acid food lists. Oxalate varies across foods, plant varieties, and picking times. To create this list, I used foods that appeared multiple times in the five sources I list below.

The Oxalic Acid Big List

Foods high in oxalic acid to be boiled or used sparingly

Vegetables
- beets
- brussels sprouts
- carrots
- collard greens
- parsley
- spinach
- sweet potato
- Swiss chard
- rhubarb

Nuts
- pecans
- peanuts

Other
- black tea
- coffee
- cocoa

Sources: Brzezinski et al. 1998; Duke 1992; Hodgkinson 1977; Chai and Liebman 2005; USDA 1984.

But do not let oxalates drive you crazy. Spinach, for instance, is high in oxalates, which bind to minerals, but it is still a very good source of folate. Here are some good rules of thumb:

1) If you eat a lot of a high-oxalate food, try to find a reasonable alternative for some of it. Not all raw vegetable juices need beets and carrots, for instance.

2) Try some wilted salads. To reduce oxalates (at the expense of some folate loss), steam spinach slightly and use as a base of a "wilted salad." Find my mom's wilted salad recipes on my Web site.

3) Learn fermentation techniques.

To-Do List: Fruit and Vegetables

• Eat fruits and vegetables that are as fresh as possible and ripe (but not overripe) to maximize the vitamin content of your diet.

• Select heirloom varieties.

• Eat local produce.

• Ferment fruits and vegetables as a regular part of your diet to improve the B vitamin content of your diet and to increase your intake of beneficial bacteria.

• To maximize the minerals you are digesting, reduce the oxalic acid in your diet by avoiding or boiling, steaming, or fermenting vegetables high in oxalates.

Cheap and Free Ways to Increase the Nutrients in Your Diet

1) **Culture and ferment**

The fermentation process increases the B vitamins in the fermented food.

2) **Use scraps for broth**

Vegetable peelings and meat scraps can be used to make soup broth. The vegetable peelings are high in nutrients. Clean the vegetable well before peeling and reserve the peels for your broth. Add bones and gristle from animal products as available to a slow cooker with water. Add salt and apple cider vinegar to draw out the minerals. I let my broth simmer for at least twelve hours but not more than twenty-four hours. It becomes bitter after a longer simmer. Stew bones for a second round to draw even more minerals out. The broth won't be as rich as the first batch, but it will have nutritional value. Read my mom's methods for vegetable and bone broths on my Web site.

3) **Soak grains**

Follow the directions in the grain chapter on preparing grains to maximize your ability to digest the minerals in them.

4) **Hunt and fish**

Wild game and fish are much higher in Omega-3 fatty acids and in other nutrients than are their conventional counterparts. They tend to be lower in saturated fats as well and have a ratio of Omega-3 to Omega-6 fats that is closer to ideal. Some lakes and rivers are stocked with fish, which make the catching easier, but these fish spent the earlier part of their lives in a tank, so you might want to seek out higher or more remote country.

5) **Forage**

In our area, purslane is a common weed, which is loaded with Omega-3 oils. Sauté purslane and scramble it with eggs. Add it to salad. Find other local "crops"—we also have "miner's lettuce," which we add to salads. Don't harvest from road sides or other areas with lots of traffic or other pollutants. Don't harvest in protected forests. The rangers will not be sympathetic to your health quest.

6) **Eat liver**

Organic liver at Whole Foods in Fresno, California, costs $2/pound. A 3-ounce serving is filling as an entrée at the cost of about forty cents. That forty cents, cooked, provides 1 mg B-6 (50 percent DRI), 260 mcg folic acid (65 percent DRI), and 83 mcg B-12 (1300 percent DRI).

✤ 12 ✤

Grains and Legumes

*I*ncreasingly, people have reduced the grains and legumes in their diets because of the low-carb movement. If that is you, you need not spend a lot of time on this chapter. The cooking techniques here in particular will be most beneficial to people on a plant-based diet of grains and legumes. The preparation strategies I outline cost nothing and will increase your absorption of minerals by about 100 percent. Here's the cheat sheet:

Cheat Sheet

- For flat breads such as tortillas, pocket bread, pizza crust, pancakes, and waffles, find sprouted or sourdough varieties.
- Find sourdough recipes for your favorite quick bread. We add some of our favorites to the Web site periodically.
- Soak your breakfast porridge or your grain dish (about 120°F with a bit of yogurt or lemon juice for two to twelve hours).
- In porridges, eat ground grains instead of whole kernels.
- Add ground wheat to your oatmeal before soaking.
- Soak legumes for eighteen hours in very warm water (140°F) before cooking.
- Eat fermented soybeans in the form of tempeh or combine your soybeans with a high-phytase grain.

Depression-Buster Grains and Legumes

I have a love–hate relationship with grains. I love them because they taste so good. I hate them because they make me chunky and sluggish. And now that I have analyzed these foods and developed a list of depression busters, that side of me that feels fat and sluggish when I eat grains was not too surprised that most of them did not make the list of depression busters, nor did a whole lot of legumes.

The bran and the germ of grains are filled with nutrients and qualify as depression busters. Lentils, fermented soybeans, cowpeas, moth beans, yard-long beans, adzuki beans, and mung beans qualify as well. But in all these cases, the preparation of these depression busters is critical. They contain a mineral inhibitor called phytic acid, which will reduce the mineral levels that you absorb. Since the mineral content of these foods is what got them on the depression buster list, they need to be prepared properly if we are to consider them depression busters.

Depression Busters

wheat bran	moth beans
wheat germ	lentils
cowpeas	adzuki beans
fermented soy	mung beans
yard-long beans	

With such a short list of grains and legumes, I should offer the same qualification here as I did in the fruit and vegetable chapter. The grains and legumes in this database probably should have more nutrients. I present data on mineral levels of organic and conventionally-grown produce in the previous chapter. The differences are striking. One of the foods from that study is wheat. The organic wheat has more than four times the magnesium as the conventionally-grown wheat. It has more than 80 percent more zinc.

All the advice in the previous chapter on buying organic, local, heirloom produce applies to grains and legumes. Your purchasing decisions could improve the vitamin and mineral content of your diet greatly.

Beyond shopping decisions, there are preparation techniques for grains and legumes that will help all those minerals from your organic garden get into your body. For no other food group is preparation as important as it is for the grain and legume families.

Nutrient Loss in Milled Grain

Most of us have gotten the memo that white flour and rice are not very healthy. Their high glycemic content can raise our blood sugar and add to our waists. They do not help us in our depression battle either—note the loss of vitamin B-6 and minerals in the table below.

Processed white flours and refined grains, including the sumptuous bed of white rice in your sushi, have been stripped of much of their nutrition. Begin to replace some of these items with the whole grain version.

Table 12.1: Refined wheat flour and nutrient loss	
	% loss (compared to whole wheat)
B-6	82.3[a]
Zinc	77.7[b]
Magnesium	84.7[b]
Iron	75.6[b]
Calcium	60.0[b]

a Schroeder 1971
b Czerniejewski et al. 1964

Phytic Acid and Mineral Absorption

In the research for this book I was struck by the solid research about phytic acid and yet the American public's relative lack of knowledge about its effects. I certainly never heard about them in my vegetarian days, yet they have profound implications for the vegetarian diet. Some nutritionists estimate that vegetarians whose primary source of protein comes from grains and legumes absorb only about 15 percent of the minerals in those foods. Based on the research I present here, that is a fair estimate, though absorption from soy-based foods is even lower. If you are a vegetarian, you can very quickly double the minerals you are absorbing by using the techniques I describe.

Phytates Matter

Whole grains and fresh legumes are problematic, unfortunately, because of their naturally high level of phytic acid, which inhibits the absorption of key minerals that we are trying to increase in our diets: iron, zinc, and magnesium specifically. Phytic acid binds to minerals in your digestive tract and escorts them out through your bowels. There will be no cell building with these minerals, even though the label on the grain or legume suggests you are eating mineral-rich food. Research has shown that phytates inhibit the absorption of significant levels of minerals in the phytate-laden food. The iron in your soybean will not help rebuild your body if you do not break down the phytic acid first.

Researchers have conducted experiments on mineral absorption that show clearly that phytates matter. A study of iron absorption in cereal porridges found in some cases a twelve-fold increase in the absorption of iron when the phytic acid was removed from the food. Participants absorbed only about 1 percent of the iron in their wheat porridge but that absorption rate increased to 12 percent when the phytic acid was removed (Hurrel et al. 2003).

Another set of experiments examined depression-fighting zinc and magnesium. Researchers provided two groups of people with bread—one group with a bread with phytates and one with a control bread with the phytates removed. Researchers then studied participants' mineral absorption via stool samples. Without phytic acid, participants absorbed about 30 percent of magnesium and zinc. With phytic acid, participants absorbed only 13 percent of their magnesium and 23 percent of their zinc (Egli et al. 2004; Bohn et al. 2004).

These results make clear that even in products lower in phytic acid, we can absorb about 50 percent more minerals if we can reduce the phytate content to zero. In higher-phytate foods such as soybeans and whole wheat, we might more than double our absorption of minerals if we can reduce the phytate levels to zero.

The Solution in Your Kitchen

Some grains and legumes are high in phytates, some are low. As a class, milled grains such as white flour are low in phytates. Do not worry about phytates in your white flour (and you are cutting back on that anyway). For our purposes here, what turns out to be the more important question is how to reduce the phytic acid content of our foods and what grains and legumes prove to be wily exceptions to these techniques.

Rise Time, Soaking, and Sprouting: Putting the enzyme phytase to work for you

For the most part, if grains and legumes are allowed to sit and stew for a while in warm water with a slightly acid medium, their phytic acid level will decline. These techniques will fight your phytates:

1) Take advantage of bread rising time. As yeast bread dough sits and is allowed to rise, the phytic acid content will be reduced. Sourdough techniques are generally the most effective if only because the rise time tends to be longer and the lactic acid in the starter breaks down the phytates.

2) Use sourdough techniques for flatbreads, quick breads, pancakes, and waffles. We turn every quick bread into a sourdough around here.

3) Soak grains for porridges. Your breakfast porridge should be soaked in advance of cooking, as should grains to be used in dishes such as tabouli. Ground grains are preferable to whole kernels since the phytic acid breaks down easier. Follow these steps:

    a. Soak in water, about equal parts water to grains (enough to cover them well).

    b. The water temperature should be between 45°C and 55°C (113°F-131°F), just above body temperature.

     c. Add an acidic ingredient to water to achieve a pH level of 4.5 to 5.5. For best results use whey, yogurt, or kefir (approximately two tablespoons per cup of grain). Otherwise add about two tablespoons of lemon juice per cup of grain.

     d. Cover with a clean dishcloth to keep the bugs out.

     e. Soak in a warm spot for at least two, and at best, twelve hours.

4) Germinate grains and legumes. Make sprouts to reduce phytic acid. Sprouted grains are used in higher-end health breads increasingly. These are great options particularly for flat breads such as tortillas and pizza crusts. Germinating will increase the folate content as well.

5) Soak your beans in very warm water (140°F) for about eighteen hours in a warm spot. I start mine one morning and cook them the following afternoon.

You will find a fairly extensive discussion of each of the above five areas on my Web site.

Oats, Corn, and Complementary Soaking

If you eat a lot of oatmeal or corn, keep reading. You need to know that the basic techniques to reduce phytates are not very effective in these two cases. Oats, corn, soy, millet, and sorghum are known to be low in phytase, the enzyme that breaks down the phytic acid. I focus on oats and corn here because they are the most common. I address soy afterward.

In a 1950 study, Mellanby reported an experiment reducing the phytic acid content of various grains, which I present in the following figure. Note that with rye and wheat it takes only two hours to reduce the phytate content under optimum conditions. With oats and corn, soaking for twelve hours is insufficient—the phytic acid levels are still about 75 percent of their original levels.

There is a fairly simple solution when making oatmeal: use about 10

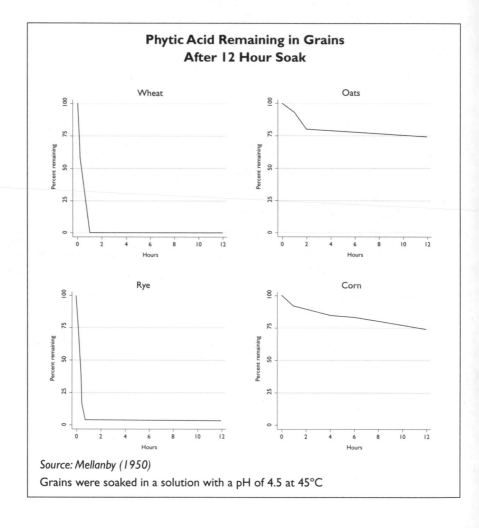

Phytic Acid Remaining in Grains After 12 Hour Soak

Source: Mellanby (1950)
Grains were soaked in a solution with a pH of 4.5 at 45°C

percent fresh ground wheat and follow the instructions I provided earlier on soaking. Grind this small amount of wheat in your coffee grinder, if you do not have a grain mill. (For larger quantities, purchase a grain mill before you burn out your coffee grinder.)

Many corn items, such as corn bread, contain wheat and, thus, make use of grain combining. However, corn products from masa such as corn tortillas, corn tortilla chips, and tamales are made from a corn dough that has been nixtamalized. The corn is soaked in lime to improve the bioavailability of niacin. This preparation process reduces the level of phytic acid by only about 20 percent (Bressani et al. 2004).

Make One Change with Breakfast

Replace your breakfast cereal with whole grain, ground porridge. Soak that porridge overnight according to the process described in this section.

You will benefit twice: (1) by replacing a processed cereal with a whole grain alternative, and (2) by reducing the phytate content of that cereal grain.

It's fast. Because of the soaking, your breakfast cereal will cook in one to two minutes, making it a fast and easy breakfast solution.

Add fat. Use butter from grass-fed cattle. The fat will help your body absorb the minerals in the cereal and will add Omega-3 fatty acids to your meal.

And when you're feeling ambitious: buy the whole grain kernel and grind your cereal grains just before soaking.

You could purchase nixtamalized corn and soak it in an acid solution to reduce the phytates further, but with limited kitchen time, your best strategy is to rely on other foods for their minerals rather than the corn product.

Soy and its Unavailable Minerals

In this house, soy products used to be a staple. We valued them for their low cost and high protein and mineral content. One of those 12-ounce tubs of tofu has 100 milligrams or so of magnesium. That is 25 percent of the DRI of magnesium. It is too bad that only about 10 milligrams are absorbed into your body. To make matters worse, there is some discussion in the nutrition literature that the phytic acid in soy may make soy protein less useable for our bodies (Reddy et al. 1989, 57–69).

A study of phytic acid in soybeans documents in detail the phytic acid level at different stages of preparation. The researchers boil the beans, pour off the water, soak them again, dehull them, steam them, drain them, and cool them. The phytic acid levels change very little with all this effort.

It is only when they ferment the beans in the form of tempeh that the phytate levels reduce to about 45 percent of the levels of the soaked soybean. Fried tempeh is an improvement still, but if the tempeh is stored for two weeks at 5°C and then fried, the researchers reached the optimal (but not perfect) reduction of the phytic acid (Sutardi and Buckle 1985). A 2003 study also found that the phytic acid level decreased by only 31 percent by fermenting soybeans (Egounlety and Aworth 2003).

Keep these results in mind as you shop for soymilk and tofu. Soybeans in soy milk are soaked, strained, and cooked. Tofu has an additional step—a coagulant is added. Both of these products retain nearly 100 percent of the phytates. Eat tempeh for a soy fix, but eat it sparingly if you do not prepare it yourself and do not know that traditional preparation methods were used. Soybean fans should learn to ferment soybeans in their own home using traditional fermentation techniques.

People who make their own soy milk and tofu might be able to improve them, if not through fermentation techniques, by soaking them with a high-phytase grain such as wheat. Researchers have combined grains and legumes strategically to reduce the phytates in one item with the phytase in another. In the case of soybeans, researchers included only 20 percent soy and 80 percent wheat. They successfully reduced the phytic acid in the porridge. Homemade milk aficionados might use a similar strategy. There is no research that I am aware of that would direct us with the proper ratio of soybeans to wheat to make a soy milk. I do not eat soy—this is an idea for experimental cooks who do.

Alternative Milks

Speaking of soy milk, phytates are a problem in all the alternative milk products available in the market place except perhaps rice milk made from white rice (which we are reducing in our diet anyway). Brown rice, nuts such as almonds, and soy all have phytic acid. If I relied on alternative milks for their nutrients, I would try to make them myself. I would use the soaking strategy for rice I outlined earlier or for nuts and seeds that I outline in the next chapter and then follow the usual process for making these milks.

Phytates Can Be Therapeutic

There is increasing discussion in research that phytates play a role in cancer prevention. Indeed, the bad news about phytates is that they inhibit mineral absorption. The good news about phytates is that they inhibit mineral absorption. Sometimes it is all about perspective. Here is the key question: What is more important for you now, increasing your body levels of magnesium and zinc or decreasing your levels of iron? For younger women reading this book, low iron is more likely a problem than high iron. For women who are post-menopausal, high iron may be a problem (but then again, low iron may still be a problem). Excess iron is implicated in disease as well and including phytates in your diet is an effective way to reduce your body's iron levels. Depending on your own circumstances and stage in the life cycle, your needs are going to be different. Pick and choose the food preparation suggestions in this chapter accordingly.

To-Do List: Grains and Legumes

- For flat breads such as tortillas, pocket bread, pizza crust, pancakes, and waffles find sprouted or sourdough varieties.
- Turn quick breads into sourdough breads using our cheaters' methods.
- Soak your breakfast porridge or your grain dish (about 120°F with a bit of yogurt or lemon juice for two to twelve hours).
- In porridges, eat ground grains instead of whole kernels.
- Add rye flakes to your oatmeal before soaking.
- Soak legumes for eighteen hours in very warm water (140°F) before cooking.
- Eat fermented soybeans in the form of tempeh or combine your soybeans with a high-phytase grain.

∽ 13 ℃

Nuts, Seeds, and Oils

*N*uts and seeds are great sources of minerals and some are high in Omega-3 fatty acids. They provide good vegetarian options for increasing the depression-busting nutrients in our diets. Here is your cheat sheet:

Cheat Sheet

- Integrate more depression-busting nuts and seeds into your diet: flax seeds, walnuts, squash seeds (including pumpkin), sesame seeds, and sunflower seeds.
- Reduce your Omega-6 to Omega-3 fatty acid ratio by consuming foods low in Omega-6 and high in Omega-3 fatty acids.
- Watch and reduce your consumption of Omega-6 fatty acids in packaged snack foods.
- Replace kitchen oils high in Omega-6 fatty acids with more favorable oils.
- Prepare your nuts and seeds to reduce their phytate content.

Depression-Buster Nuts and Seeds

The USDA database includes six depression-buster nuts and seeds. Note that flax seeds, walnuts, squash seeds, sesame seeds, and sunflower seeds are high in some combination of our depression-fighting minerals, vitamins, and fatty acids.

Notable for their Omega-3 content are flax seeds and walnuts, which have high levels of the Omega-3 alpha lipoic acid (ALA). All our depression busters are good sources of minerals. The only caveat is that they also have a high phytate content, which will reduce the minerals you absorb. The flax seeds and walnuts could make the depression-buster list almost solely by virtue of their ALA content, but the other depression buster seeds really should only make the list if they are prepared to reduce their phytate content. I discuss preparation methods later in this chapter.

The salad recipes I provide in the Appendix, integrate these nuts and seeds liberally. If nuts and seeds are some of the only depression busters in your diet, you should use them fairly liberally as well. The depression buster list is based on 100 grams of each food item, which translates into about 1 cup of walnut pieces, ⅔ cup of sesame seeds or sunflower seeds, and ½ cup of flax seeds or squash seeds.

But in eating large quantities of nuts, consider their oil content. Sesame and sunflower seeds are great additions to salads, but in their oil form, they do have a high content of Omega-6 fatty acids. I recommend them as salad toppers and snack foods but not in their oil form.

Depression Busters

flax seeds	sesame seeds
walnuts	sunflower seeds
squash seeds (pumpkin)	

The sesame and sunflower seeds and their oils bring up an important issue for the fight against depression: we need to find high mineral and vitamin food sources, rich in Omega-3 fatty acids but also not too high in Omega-6 fatty acids. While Omega-6 fatty acids are essential to human health, they are so common in the food that we have available to us that all you need is one indiscretion at an office lunch party to give you plenty of Omega-6 oils. A meal out—almost any meal out, anywhere—will help you meet your Omega-6 requirement. Grain-fed beef, pork, and poultry are high in Omega-6 fatty acids. Any convenience food "snack" item such as chips, crackers, and pastries will more than fill your quota. Omega-6 fatty acids are all around us and we will be challenged to meet the Omega-6 to Omega-3 fatty acid ratio of our ancestors.

Oil Storage

Store all of your Omega-3 rich oils in your refrigerator. Cod liver oil, fish oil, and flax seed oil can all go rancid quickly. Follow the directions on the label regarding the expiration date and storage of the product.

The Omega-6 to Omega-3 Ratio in Oils

Our ancestors ate a ratio of Omega-6 to Omega-3 fatty acids of about 1:1. Some researchers estimate that the standard American diet has a ratio of 15:1 or higher. Research shows that we can fight depression by increasing our intake of Omega-3 fatty acids, but it may also be therapeutic to decrease our Omega-6 intake to get us closer to the Omega-6 to Omega-3 ratio of days gone by.

One way to think about this change is simply to incorporate foods with a more favorable Omega-6 to Omega-3 ratio. Foods with a favorable Omega-6 to Omega-3 ratio include any kind of fish oil, flaxseed oil, and of course, the fish and seeds they are derived from.

Yet the ratio is not the entire story when it comes to food selection. We can select foods low in the Omega-6 to Omega-3 ratio, but we should also select foods with an absolute level of Omega-6 that is low. Olive oil, for instance, has an Omega-6 to Omega-3 ratio that is just "okay." It is about 13:1. But the fact is, it has very little Omega-6 or Omega-3—it is primarily an Omega-9 oil. So even with an Omega-6 to Omega-3 ratio that is not great, olive oil will do you no harm in your goal of reducing your overall Omega-6 to Omega-3 ratio in your diet.

Note the oils in the following table. I have categorized them according to their Omega-6 to Omega-3 ratio (low, medium, or high) and according to their absolute level of Omega-6 (low, medium, or high). If you work on reducing the oils in your diet that are in the lower right-hand corner—a high ratio of Omega-6 to Omega-3 and a high level of Omega-6—your Omega-6 to Omega-3 intake will be closer to that of your ancestors. The oils shaded in gray are the ticket to improving your overall ratio. These are oils with a low ratio and a low level of Omega-6 fatty acids. So if you are replacing oils in your diet and you find that olive oil works for you as a good substitute for corn oil, by all means make the change today.

Table 13.1: Best oils for reducing your Omega-6 to Omega-3 ratio
Shaded oils are either low in Omega-6 or have a low Omega-6 to Omega-3 ratio

	Low ratio (under 5:1)	Medium ratio (5:1 to 15:1)	High ratio (above 15:1)
Low Omega-6 (under 500 mg/tbs)	salmon oil cod liver oil herring oil sardine oil butter oil		coconut oil
Medium Omega-6 (500–3000 mg/tbs)	flaxseed oil canola oil mustard oil	olive oil	palm oil shortening (industrial) sunflower
High Omega-6 (above 3000 mg/tbs)		walnut oil soybean oil wheat germ oil	mayonnaise (soy+safflower) rice bran oil corn oil sesame oil cottonseed oil grapeseed oil peanut oil sunflower oil

Based on data from the National Institutes of Health

There is a great deal of research on oils because of the importance of our oil choice in our overall health. The Omega-6 to Omega-3 content is one key issue we should consider. There are other issues as well and selecting a healthy oil for cooking or for salads is fairly complicated.

Cooking Oil Choices

Olive oil. While this oil will not help your Omega-3 levels, it will not hurt your Omega-6 to Omega-3 balance. The extra virgin form is loaded with polyphenols, which can help protect your body against cancer and heart disease. It is best used raw but can be used in low heat cooking.

Canola oil. This oil has a fairly high smoke point and a high Omega-3 content. The oil is generally accepted as quite healthy, though there is some controversy surrounding it. Studies have used stroke-prone rats and fed them diets with either canola or soy oil as their exclusive dietary fat. The canola rats develop stroke symptoms sooner and die sooner than the soybean oil rats (Ohara et al. 2006; Naito et al. 2003). But despite these studies, organic expeller-pressed canola oil is recommended by most nutritionists as a good pick.

Butter and coconut oil. The controversy in these oils lies in their saturated fat content. As a survivor of the low-fat diet craze of the 1980s, I do not worry about saturated fat all that much anymore. It is not yet clear in the literature how much we need, though humans have survived for millennia on at least a bit of saturated fat. Coconut also has antioxidant properties.

Recommendations:
- Oil for frying. Avoiding fried foods altogether is your best bet, but I have been known to use coconut oil on occasion for frying.
- Oil for baking. There are baked goods that require shortening. The trans fats in the shortening will interfere with Omega-3 metabolism and they may play a role in heart disease and cancer. Coconut oil performs very well as a replacement for shortening. In some recipes, butter may work well.
- Oil for sautés. Olive oil for a low-heat dish is your best bet. If the dish includes a meat, the fat from that meat may be enough to fry

the vegetables. Add water or a bit of oil to keep it from sticking. Depending on the direction of canola oil research, it could be a very good stir fry option.

Salad Oils

Perhaps we eat so many salads because the oil decision is much easier to make. Salads are also easy to prepare, so it is hard to go wrong.

Flaxseed, mustard, canola, and olive oils can all be used raw in a salad. My choice is a combination of flaxseed and olive oil—flaxseed for the Omega-3 fatty acids and olive oil for the known antioxidant properties. The big issue you will face with these oils is developing a nose for rancidity.

If you do not know what rancid oils smell like, buy nuts in a quick stop gas station. Find a very dusty bag of nuts. Buy the bag, open it, and if the nuts smell strange, you have your example of rancid oil. Throw the nuts away or keep them as a reminder of the smell. Do not consume your kitchen oil if it smells "off."

PHYTATES IN NUTS AND SEEDS

In the grain and legumes chapter we saw that grains and legumes contain phytic acid and that the phytic acid binds to iron, magnesium, and zinc in our digestive tract and keeps those key depression-fighting minerals from being absorbed in our bodies. We absorb about half of the minerals we would otherwise absorb if we could remove all the phytic acid. Nuts and seeds, just like the seed heads of wheat and barley, contain phytic acid as well. As with grains, roasting will reduce the phytic acid content to some degree, but soaking or germinating them is a better strategy.

There is little research on the most effective methods for reducing the phytates in nuts and seeds, so we must make inferences from what we know about grains since grains are the seeds of various grasses. We know from the grain research that it is much more difficult to reduce the phytate content of a whole kernel of grain compared to ground grain.

Table 13.2: Phytate content of nuts and seeds

	mg phytate/100 g
Chestnuts	47[a]
Walnuts (English)	760[a]
Peanut butter	1,252[b]
Sunflower seeds	1,606[c]
Sesame seeds	1,616[c]
Brazil nuts	1,799[a]
Cashews	1,866[b]
Pumpkin seeds	1,889[c]

a McCance and Widdowson 1978
b Oberleas and Harland 1981
c Harland and Oberleas 1987

To reduce the phytic acid, there are three general methods depending on the product you are trying to make:

1) Soak the whole nuts or seeds just as you would your grains. Strain them. Spread them on a cookie sheet and roast them in your oven on the lowest possible temperature. After about twenty-four hours you will have a very crunchy nut that tastes better than any roasted nut you can buy.

2) Germinate the nut or seed: soak overnight, drain soaking water, rinse nuts or seeds, sprout in sprouting environment for two days or more. Before the tails get longer than you desire, dry them out in your oven for about twenty-four hours for a good crunch, or let them continue to germinate and use them as sprouts. See instructions in the Appendix.

3) Grind the nuts slightly before soaking. Follow the directions in (1) to dry the nuts out. I use this method for making almond butter. I don't grind them into flour. I just increase the surface area of the nut in my food processor and then soak them and dry them. They dry much more quickly than

the whole nut and I immediately turn them into nut butter. I would not go to this much trouble if it were not for my son who, on some days, lives only on this food item.

If you are drying the nuts and seeds (not just making sprouts), dry them in a food dehydrator or in an oven at a low temperature to preserve the enzymes. This method will help with your overall digestion. During the summer I actually put cookie sheets of nuts on my car in the full sun. I cover them with sheer fabric to keep the birds away and bring them in at night to keep the raccoons off them. My kitchen does not heat up as a result and I save some fossil fuel.

To-Do List: Nuts, Seeds, and Oils

- Integrate more depression-busting nuts and seeds into your diet: flax seeds, walnuts, squash seeds (including pumpkin), sesame seeds, and sunflower seeds.
- Reduce your Omega-6 to Omega-3 fatty acid ratio by consuming foods low in Omega-6 and high in Omega-3 fatty acids.
- Watch and reduce your consumption of Omega-6 fatty acids in packaged snack foods.
- Replace kitchen oils high in Omega-6 fatty acids with more favorable oils.
- Prepare your nuts and seeds to reduce their phytate content.

~ 14 ~

Getting Started

I have done my time on diets. I can be strict and diligent when need be. I am often compulsive about the nutrition in my diet, for better or for worse. The compulsion part probably saps me of a nutrient or two, but increasingly it is my philosophy that we just need to make things better, not perfect. Over the many years of our lives, if we keep making things better, we may end up eating a highly nutritious diet. Now is not the time to worry about the end point. Now is the time to make improvements.

We all need to cut processed foods out of our diets and replace them with foods rich in depression-fighting nutrients. This is not easy in any way, but neither is being debilitated by depression. The time and energy that a diet change takes is worth it. You just need to establish a pace you can manage.

Five Things You Can Do This Week

1. Find sources of supplemental Omega-3 fatty acids and B vitamins. As your diet improves, these supplements may not be necessary but they may provide you with some short-term relief as you make over your diet.

2. Add a couple of salads to your menu for the week. Add a soup. Note from the information that follows how easy they are to make.

3. Buy free-range or Omega-3 eggs, if you eat eggs.

4. If you are working and eating lunch out, brown-bag it a day or two a week. Plan leftovers in your daily menus to help fill

up your lunch box. Buy a really cool lunch box that will make you popular at the office.

5. If you eat cereal, follow the cereal meal makeover suggestion in the Appendix.

ADD SALADS TO YOUR MENUS

None of us really has much time to cook. Even in our house where we make a point of eating home-cooked foods, keeping salads on the menu as single entrée meals saves us when we are very busy and pinched for kitchen preparation time.

Most salads may require no cooking at all. They are simple and nutritious. All they arc is lettuce and "stuff." And actually, some salads are just "stuff." Keep lettuce around and a variety of "stuff" (preferably of the depression-buster food variety) and you will be set.

If you brown-bag it to work, salads are a great option. Use some of the following strategies:

- Buy lettuce at the farmers' market—local, fresh lettuce. Ask them about heirloom varieties and tell them why you are interested.
- Prepare the lettuce in batches: clean lettuce for two to three lunches for the week. Put the leaves in a plastic bag, not entirely sealed, to allow the lettuce to breathe. Refrigerate it. Tear the lettuce when you are ready to put the salad together.
- Use depression-busting protein toppings: salmon, walnuts, sunflower seeds, sesame seeds, tuna, and beef.
- Make a depression-busting salad dressing: splash on some flaxseed and olive oil and a touch of red wine vinegar.

Create Your Own Vinaigrette Dressing

Using a combination of olive oil and flaxseed oil, you can make a tasty dressing for any salad. I do not usually keep a prepared dressing in the refrigerator (though it is a great treat when I do); I just splash oil, vinegar, salt, and pepper on the lettuce and toss the salad. I add salad toppers and then a bit more oil and vinegar.

Salad dressings used to intimidate me until my mom started teaching me what ingredients go with what foods. Once I understood that, I graduated from following salad dressing recipes slavishly to adding a dash of something here and there. The key is in your oil and vinegar selection.

Selecting Oils: Olive and Flaxseed

Buy the finest, freshest olive oil and flaxseed oil you can find. Extra virgin olive oil has a strong flavor and you may prefer to start with a lighter olive oil to become accustomed to the flavor. Switch to extra virgin later. Store the olive oil in a cool, dark place and store the flaxseed oil in the refrigerator. Both can go rancid.

Selecting Vinegars: Learn the Difference

Fine vinegars are the secret to fine salad dressings. Your choice will depend on your salad.

- **Starter vinegar:** white wine or rice vinegar. These vinegars have a light fragrance that goes with any foods and will not overpower delicate foods such as chicken and white fish. Rice vinegar is a bit sweeter than white wine vinegar.
- **Red wine vinegar.** Red wine vinegar will add a bit of red color to your lettuce and a more intense flavor than the white wine vinegar. Use this vinegar with salad toppings such as red meat and fatty fish that have intense flavors of their own.
- **Balsamic vinegar.** Use balsamic vinegar as you would red wine vinegar, but keep in mind that you do not need nearly as much. Add a tablespoon or two to a regular dressing made with one of the wine vinegars. The flavor is fantastic.

Put the Dressing Together

- Mix together one part olive oil and one part flax oil in a jar with a tight-fitting lid. If you have a large family, plan on making a quart or more dressing at a time.
- Add one part vinegar of your choice.
- Add about one clove of freshly-chopped garlic per each one-half cup of oil.
- Add salt and freshly ground pepper to taste.
- Shake well and pour over a salad.

From this basic vinaigrette you can make many different types of salad dressings. My mom has some suggestions on the Web site for making your own signature dressings. You can also do what I do most of the time—splash on oil, salt, pepper, and whatever vinegar suits my fancy.

Keep Salad Ingredients on Hand

Salad greens
romaine lettuce (best for freshness)
arugula (to add some spice)
escarole (for color and texture)

Complementary salad vegetables
fresh garlic
green onions
red onions
tomatoes in season
anything in season

Complementary salad toppings
depression-buster nuts and seeds
depression-buster meats

Salad dressing ingredients
olive oil
flaxseed oil
lemons
red and white wine vinegars
balsamic vinegar

Simmer Some Soups

There are days when I have tight deadlines, no time to cook, and need good food to keep my mental focus. Broth alone or a simple soup is a good solution.

Buy a bag of bones from the butcher and put them on the stove or in a slow cooker to simmer throughout the day. Cover them with water and add a couple splashes of vinegar. Add a handful of fresh parsley and a bay leaf. Depending on what you plan to do with your broth, add a quartered onion and a couple cloves of garlic, or dried, granulated garlic. Let the broth simmer for up to twelve hours (but at least three). Simmering for much longer will cause the broth to be bitter.

After simmering, strain off the broth and make your soup. Your soup can be as simple as a bowl of salted broth, salted broth with an egg added and beaten when the soup is hot ("egg drop soup"), or broth with some nutritious greens. Each of these "soups" will take less time to prepare than it will take you to order in or drive to a restaurant.

Six Uses for Broth
By Jeanie Rose, a.k.a. Mom

If you have not experienced homemade broth in your cooking, you must make an effort to do so. Broth adds a richness that is difficult to describe and that everyone deserves to experience. After you have savored your last delectable spoonful of soup, know that you are building your health.

1. Season and consume your broth as a hot drink with any meal or as an energy-giving snack.

2. Use the broth as a base for a vast array of thin or thick soups and stews.
3. Use it as a base for gravies and sauces to go on vegetables, meats, and even salads.
4. Braise vegetables in a small amount of stock and then consume both the vegetables and the cooking liquid.
5. If your stir fry calls for added liquid, add broth.
6. Use as the cooking liquid for grains, beans, and pasta.

My mom adds new soup recipes to the Web site regularly and has detailed instructions on making vegetable and bone broth. She is a soup connoisseur.

Nuts and Seeds Instead of Crackers

Crackers and chips are fun snacks but they are high in Omega-6 fatty acids and do not have a lot of nutrients to offer. Nuts or seeds are better choices. They, too, are high in Omega-6 fatty acids but are also fairly mineral rich. They are a good snack alternative when you are facing the crackers and chips.

- Carry nuts in your backpack for a quick snack. Put them in your lunchbox and keep them in the console of your car when traveling.
- Use nuts and seeds for entertaining. After the party when the snacks linger for a week, you will save yourself a bit of cracker and chip eating.
- Sesame seeds are the most versatile of seeds. Keep a supply on hand to sprinkle on salads, vegetables, meats, casseroles, soups, and omelets.

Learn Some Healthful Food Preparation Techniques

Nature provides us with some exceptional ways to add value to the food we are eating. Begin to experiment with traditional food preparation techniques.

- **Culture and ferment your food.**
  Make your own yogurt or kefir. Culture vegetables. Make your own fermented sodas. See the Appendix for these very easy techniques.
- **Soak your grains and legumes in advance.**
  They will cook faster and you will absorb more nutrients that are naturally present in the food.

- **Experiment with sourdough techniques.**

  Make cakes, quick breads, and any bread using traditional sourdough methods. If you bake at all, this will be an easy transition. See the Appendix for basic instructions.

FIND YOUR FOOD SOURCES

You can make many positive changes in your eating simply by changing the types of food you are buying. Your local farmers' market is likely to have fresher produce than the grocery store and you might even find more nutrient-rich heirloom varieties.

- **Visit farmers' markets.**

  For me, just visiting a farmers' market is a mood lifter. The smell of fresh produce and all the cool people I meet there make it a memorable event. Buy your fresh produce at your local farmers' market. Even if it's not organic, fresh produce may have a higher nutrient content than produce that has traveled to the grocery store. Buy heirloom varieties when you can find them. Even if the nutrients are the same as in modern varieties, the heirlooms tend to be much more flavorful.

- **Improve your eggs.**

  Changing the eggs you eat is a very simple change. You may end up spending more money if you go the Omega-3 enriched route. But with enough hunting locally you may be able to find a good egg at a reasonable price.

  > **Free range.** While you're at the farmers' market, keep an eye out for eggs and ask if the hens are allowed to range outside of their hen house.

  > **Omega-3 enriched.** Buy Omega-3 enriched eggs, available at nearly every grocery store.

  > **Grow your own.** Most cities will allow you to have a few hens in your yard. If you have the space, consider this as

a food-cost saving measure. Whether you do this will depend a lot on your sense of adventure. Hens do not tend to know the difference between scratch areas and pristine landscaping. Gardeners with more pristine yards may want to shop for eggs at the market.

• **Research meats.**

Coming from a nearly meat-free background, the meat research took me a while. Not only did I not know how to cook it, I did not even know what to look for or ask for. What I did at first was spend a ridiculous amount of money at health food stores. I love health food stores, but I cannot afford to buy meat there regularly.

What I have managed to do is find local ranchers who raise the animals. I buy them live and hire a butcher and processor to do all the dirty work. For beef, I split the purchase with a friend and we have more than we can possibly eat in a year. If you live in beef country, this could be a very good option for you. You will find stories of my meat-buying adventures on my blog, should you decide to take this path. But for general retail purchases, here are some options:

> **Pastured meat.** Eat Wild (http://www.eatwild.com) provides a geographic listing of suppliers of pastured meat. You can purchase meat via mail order. Shipments are packed frozen. Here are a couple:
>
> • Paidom Meats (http://www.paidom.com)
>
> • Lasater Beef (http://www.lasatergrasslandsbeef.com)
>
> **Wild fish and seafood.** Become familiar with the fish and seafood offerings in your area. As I mentioned in the meat and seafood chapter, you can find good research sources on the Internet. The Web site of the Monterey Bay Aquarium (http://www.mbayaq.org/cr/seafoodwatch.asp) provides a list of fish available in each region of the country. These fish are grown or harvested in a sustainable fashion.
>
> Ocean's Alive (http://www.oceansalive.org) provides lists of fish and environmental pollutants.

I take this fish and seafood information into local Mexican grocery stores, where I find some exceptional deals. The stores here are very good at displaying the food's origin. So with a check against the Ocean's Alive data, I feel pretty good about buying something that I might otherwise wonder about.

As with other meats, you can also buy seafood via mail order. Here are a couple of vendors:

Fishhugger (http://www.fishhugger.com)

Vital Choice Seafood (http://www.vitalchoice.com)

• **Pastured dairy**

It would be great if I could just say, "Buy an organic milk because the organic standards require that lactating cows be pastured." Apparently it is not quite as easy as that these days. There are lawsuits against some large organic milk companies because those operations purportedly do not allow their cows access to pasture. While this book was in press, one large dairy lost its certification and I created a video eulogy in its honor.

You can keep up with this issue at a dairy watchdog site provided by The Cornucopia Institute at http://www.cornucopia.org.

Cornucopia also ranks dairies from one to five cows. A rating of "five cows" generally means that cows have access to pasture throughout the year and the company does not sell to large chain stores. You might check out how your local dairies are ranked. If they are ranked low, give them a ring and get their side of the story.

As with any food item, your best bet is to ask around in your community. On your driving expeditions, look for the black and white cows (or the brown Jerseys). Talk to the staff at your health food store.

• **Oils**

Reduce your use of high Omega-6 vegetable oils by replacing them with olive oil for low-heat cooking and adding flax and olive oil in raw food preparations.

- **Baked goods**

   Good bread companies tend to be regional, so it is difficult to create a general list of good products. Start reading labels when you have a few extra minutes. Buy real sourdough bread that uses whole grain flour or sprouted grains. Check the label: if it has baker's yeast in it, it is not a traditional sourdough, even if it is labeled as a sourdough. Sprouted grain products are great for flatbreads like tortillas and pizza crust. Whole Foods carries great sprouted products from Alvarado Street Bakery and Food for Life. Consider making your own as well. Look for Mom's instructions on the Web site.

- **Start your own garden.**

   Most people can have some sort of garden in the spring through fall. They are great for exercise and some of the sun exposure will help your body produce vitamin D. (A half hour of exposure is typically good. Beyond that, you may need to cover up.)

- **Pay wholesale—join a food co-op.**

   Co-ops offer wholesale prices on organic and whole-foods items. Here are a handful of co-ops that operate in different regions of the United States:

   - United Buying Clubs, eastern and midwestern United States, (http://www.unitedbuyingclubs.com)
   - United Natural Foods, Incorporated, in certain parts of the United States (http://www.unfi.com)
   - Azure Standard, northwest United States and Southern California (http://www.azurestandard.com)

I provide a lot of information in the previous food chapters. Don't try to implement all the possible changes today. It's not reasonable to do so. The first step you can take is to make over the foods that you are already eating. Choose your favorite items and most-eaten dishes and improve their ingredients.

MAKE SMALL CHANGES AND
BREAK THE CYCLE OF DEPRESSION

Food matters a great deal to our overall health and certainly to our mental health. It is easy, however, to become complacent and believe that with advances in technology and with the richest and cheapest food supply in human history that we will never have to worry about food.

My grandpa used to have to find work each morning to make sure his family had dinner that night. Grandpa had a food access problem. We have a food choice problem. Our freedom to choose allows us to make bad decisions about what to eat. We also tend to make bad decisions about where food lies in our list of priorities. I make bad decisions just about every day, but I am making fewer bad decisions as time marches on.

The intent of this chapter is to help you begin to make choices that should alleviate your depression over the many thousands of days you have left. It is fairly simple each day to add nutrients to the meals you are used to eating. Spend some time looking around to see what basic things you can change. Replace something in your diet every week or every month with a more nutritious alternative. Write to me to report on your most interesting makeovers. Send me some new menu makeover challenges.

∽ 15 ᗡ

Conclusion

*E*very generation in every era has social movements that respond to the crisis of the day. The women of my great grandmother's generation fought for suffrage, my grandmother's generation fought against the global aspirations of the Nazi party, and my mother's generation fought against the war in Vietnam.

In 2030 as we look back on the early part of the twenty-first century, we will reflect on social movements advocating for natural foods grown locally, without the use of herbicides and pesticides, and without genetic modifications. Along with these important movements, which in themselves will help us rebuild from depression, the time is here for us to be proactive about depression itself.

THE YEAR 2030

The World Health Organization (WHO) predicts that in less than a quarter of a century, depression will be the second-greatest cause of disability adjusted life years (DALYs)—years lost from our work, from our families, from our lives, all due to depression. This forecast in itself is discouraging. We have already lost too many years to depression. But the news is actually a bit worse than that.

The forecast model developed by the WHO assumes that rates of depression will remain constant over time. It assumes that a sixty-year-old woman here in the United States in 2030 will suffer at the same rate as a sixty-year-old woman in 2002. The model assumes that economic circumstances will change, global distribution of people will change, and those changes will impact rates of disease overall. It is those more general social changes that will put depression in second place.

But actually other research suggests that a sixty-year-old woman in 2030 is likely to suffer much more from depression than a sixty-year-old in 2002. Depression rates are increasing across age groups, not remaining constant. As we discussed in chapter 6, each new generation of Americans is increasingly likely to suffer from depression.

Worse still, we know that nutritional deficiencies are associated with other diseases as well as with depression. Depressed people are more likely to develop heart disease, possibly because of the Omega-3 fatty acid deficiency well documented in both diseases. So not only are we likely to struggle with many more years of depression, but we will increasingly fight other diseases as well.

And all this is to say that if we do not do something to alleviate our own depression and to help our children, their children, our parents, and our husbands, 2030 will be a very bad year. It will be far worse than data analysts at the WHO suggest to us.

If we do not make changes, the decades leading up to 2030 will be filled with longer depressive slumps and shorter periods of functional days. The younger generations in our families are likely to struggle even more.

Sixty-One in 2030

We do not often celebrate birthdays in this family, but we will be having a very big birthday party in 2030. I will turn sixty-one that year and I will be the age of my grandmother when she died of complications from postpartum depression. As I have mentioned, her depression started in her years as a young mother and stole decades of life from her as she struggled to raise her children. Her children became teenagers and then adults as she struggled with depression, developed diabetes and heart disease, and died of a stroke at the age of sixty-one.

Depression should have been her wake-up call, but she did not realize its association with nutrition. She did not realize that with nutrient deficiencies left unchecked, her body would fall victim to other diseases. Instead she was left to suffer for many years, and she never had the quality of life that we all deserve.

So 2030 will be an important year for me and for all of us. Decades full of days between now and then will help us change the trend of ever-increasing years lost to depression.

We have tools to improve our nutrition and our lifestyles so that every day we wake up, our own likelihood of depression is lower than it would have been otherwise. Every day we wake up, the severity of our depression will be less than it would have been otherwise.

Unlike my grandmother's generation, we can at least take the edge off depression with the knowledge that we have. We know a great deal:

- Nutrients matter; deficiencies can make us depressed.
- Supplementing with dietary nutrients eases depression in clinical trials.
- We know how to ask our doctors to test for nutrient deficiencies.
- We can shop for food supplements using current research.
- We can select and prepare our food so that we are getting more of our meals.

We have many tools and we need to begin, slowly, to implement them starting today. To take on this task of changing depression trend lines, we need to do three things.

1. Spend thirty seconds or less on "what I should have done differently."

We all reflect on it and there are many decades of bad decisions in our families. My grandmother did not know the impact of her diet choices. My mother cringes over the peanut butter diet of her pregnancy with me. I reflect on the impact of all my fad diets. The rate of depression is increasing so rapidly, in part, because so many of us have made bad decisions. What you can do today (after reflecting for thirty seconds or less on the bad decisions) is to begin to make good decisions.

2. Make one change on every good day.

Depression is insidious, partly because it steals our power. We are overwhelmed and immobilized and cannot see our way clear to change anything on bad days. Those bad days are not the days to make changes. We need to leverage the good days to make the bad days less bad. As we have good days, we can implement a small change that will help us on bad days.

- Buy a good kitchen ingredient to replace a bad one. Replace the corn oil with olive oil and improve your Omega-3 to Omega-6 fatty acid ratio.
- Find a healthier convenience food to replace your least healthy convenience foods.
- Shop at a farmers' market. Find some old-fashioned varieties of produce grown in your area. They are likely to be higher in nutrients.
- Learn to make kefir sodas to replace your regular sodas. You will save money and add B vitamins to your diet.
- Ferment extra summer squash and, thereby, add enzymes and B vitamins to your diet.

As you begin to feel better, make small changes at a quicker pace. Make a big change on occasion. None of us will lack the opportunity to make changes between now and 2030. Some of us will make changes at a slower pace than others, but none of us will lack projects. You can follow my changes on my blog.

3. Help your family and friends

Daughters, mothers, and grandmothers have the power to change a family. We should start with ourselves first. As we have the energy, we can help the rest of the family live a healthier lifestyle. If you are cooking for a family, those meals can be improved to include more nutrients. All meals can be tweaked—the meal makeovers in the Appendix provide some examples. Meals do not have to be complicated or perfect, just better than they would have been. Keep improving them as you are able. Everyone in the household will benefit.

If your children or grandchildren are out of the house, cook them some depression-fighting foods. No one I know would begrudge a home-cooked meal. No one has ever turned down my kefir sodas either.

Help your depressed friends and family see the link between depression and nutrition. Help them identify the nutrients they need. Shop for their supplements or food. A young woman I know is on seven medications for depression and substance abuse. It is her goal to be on just one medication. Her family has helped her by recognizing her need for Omega-3 fatty acids, magnesium, and zinc, providing them for her, and helping her remember to take them. They provided her with the most absorbable form of the minerals, knowing that she would not take them as often as intended. She has a long road ahead of her but has started to make changes with the help of her family. Some day she will be able to make changes for herself.

As your family members and friends feel better, help them begin to make small changes on their good days. Between now and 2030, we will be able to make a powerful number of small changes in our lives. Take it at a pace you can manage, but start today. And may we all be blessed with long lives filled with increasing numbers of good days.

ʃome years back my mother and I engaged in one of those hypothetical conversations: "At the end of your life, if you were given the chance to spend fifteen minutes with your child at any age in her life cycle would you spend fifteen minutes with her as an adult or fifteen minutes rocking her as a newborn baby?" My mother responded easily, "Definitely the adult version. We would have a much more interesting conversation." Mom was surprised by my answer: I chose the newborn version of Frederick.

Nearly seven years and time in therapy has not erased the loss I feel over Frederick's newborn days. What I do remember of his infancy is not something I cherish. I remember comforting him, concerned that he was infested with demons. I remember his screams piercing the night. I remember the pillow that would have ended the screams quickly, but luckily has finished its own life in a municipal waste dump. We all made it out alive, but we did miss the opportunity to sit still together and to find comfort in each other. A baby rocked by his mother is less anxious than one lying alone. Surely a mother is less anxious when she is rocking her baby. I have grieved deeply over our loss of those months.

Months of loss became years and the depression taxed our family structure. It stole our time together. It stole our money. Knowing that these situations typically get worse rather than better in subsequent pregnancies, no one in this household was brave enough to plan another child, though we all wanted one more than just about anything else. Much to our surprise, I spent the better part of 2008 pregnant and putting this book even further behind deadline.

The pregnancy was physically difficult with my advancing age but I managed to keep my sanity even through difficult times. Some of the ups and downs are memorialized on the Rebuild Blog. We hosted a beautiful formal wedding on our property for 200 people in my second trimester. I faced problems in my for-pay work in my third trimester that would have taxed my brain under any circumstances. We planned for the bad times to hit hard in the third trimester when I had major depression and psychotic episodes the first time around. As grace and good preparation would have it, I avoided down cycles entirely.

As the pregnancy came to an end, I began to think that this baby was my second chance: maybe I could enjoy my baby like many people seem to do. Maybe I would get my baby-rocking time after all. I wondered if I would have a boy who would look just like Frederick as an infant, though the entire family and friendship circle was expecting a girl.

The end of the pregnancy became increasingly difficult as climbing out of bed turned into a gymnastic event and my blood pressure teetered on the verge of hypertension. The hypertension may have been pregnancy-induced. It may have been induced by the demons in my head concerned about a repeat Cesarean section and, more so, about the possibility of having a baby with health problems. My blood pressure climbed each day in the week leading up to the birthday and my anxiety climaxed as I was wheeled through a hospital hallway and into the surgery room. It was a hallway in which I felt abandoned nearly seven years before, recovering from thoughts that I was dying from surgery and not understanding where my baby and family were. After passing through the hallway this time around, the surgery team worked hard to distract me from my own anxiety for the twenty-two minutes it took for baby to be birthed.

After twenty-two minutes of extreme anxiety, an amazing thing happened in that operating room: I gave birth to a healthy baby who looked just like Frederick. Someone on the surgery team exclaimed, "It's a boy!" My husband examined him and reported back to me, "He's beautiful!" I cried so much for no apparent reason that the anesthesiologist spiked my spinal medication with a calming elixir. She assumed my emotions were due to anxiety.

We are home now, still in the early newborn stage, and I hold this baby most of the day. I take in every little sound he makes. There does not seem to be a way to both enjoy and record every moment of this time for posterity, though I have tried.

For as well as it is going, I am well aware that I am living on the razor's edge with built-in sleep deprivation, hormonal shifts, nutrient depletion, and facing the worst economy I have lived through. Every day I focus on keeping myself out of the pit. Every day, "sanity" is a win.

While my focus is on survival and enjoying my children, I do post occasionally on the Rebuild Blog about my survival strategies. The depression struggle is complex and a long game, lasting over a lifetime. I share my game with you in this book and on the blog, hoping that you will find a tool or two to assist you in winning yours.

~ ACKNOWLEDGMENTS C~

*T*his book began as a short memoir to help me process my experience. Soon the book became a research project to help me in my own health struggles. The research took one year; the book as a whole took two years.

Over those two years my husband, Sander, and my mom, Jeanie, provided me with great support. They read far more drafts than any person should. They took turns taking my son on trips to the Central Coast, Magic Mountain, and children's museums across Southern California to provide me with time and space to concentrate. My son, Frederick, made his own sacrifices. As the book heads to production Frederick says, "Mama, now *you* can take me to Magic Mountain."

Over those two years, the librarians at California Polytechnic State University at San Luis Obispo provided me with access to a great collection of food science literature and a very generous interlibrary loan staff for all of the odds and ends articles I consulted along the way.

The research in this book crosses at least three disciplines and benefited from comments of our friend Adelise Gallion, RN, who read an early draft and made painstaking comments. Annell Adams, MD contributed to the book but also served as the content editor. Annell is busy treating postpartum women by day and took time from her own family to make many positive contributions to this book.

Friends Jane, Youngiee, Elisabeth, Carren, and Valerie made many beneficial comments as well. Fred Vogt and Larry Grote made conceptual and grammatical suggestions. Jill MacCorkle and Collette Leonard did a meticulous final read of the manuscript and saved me from many embarrassments. Of course for errors, omissions, and any sort of bad writing that remains, you can thank me.

I had a team of health care professionals who assisted me at various stages in my own recovery. They helped shape my plan to rebuild from depression.

The physical beauty of the book is a result of Peter Holm's great talent. Look for him at Sterling Hill Productions in Vermont.

Appendix

Nutrient Testing Information

Most values in blood work are controversial. The reference ranges are based on population statistics, so if you are below about the fifth percentile you may be considered deficient. Many doctors in complementary medicine believe that a large percentage of the population is deficient and if you are in the bottom five percent (which is what a score at the fifth percentile or below represents), you are in major trouble. Many doctors in complementary medicine, then, will treat people who are borderline as well.

B Vitamins

A generally recognized indirect measure of your status of folate, B-12, and B-6 is the *plasma homocysteine* test. This test will be available through your doctor and it will likely be covered by your insurance, if you have insurance.

A high value on the plasma homocysteine test is a warning sign to you. It suggests you may be low in at least one of these B vitamins, it puts you at risk of heart disease, and it is associated with depression. Pregnant women who supplement their diets with folic acid should have homocysteine levels of eight or less; without a folic acid supplement pregnant women should score ten or below. Non-pregnant adults who supplement should score twelve or below and those who do not supplement should score fifteen or below (Refsum et al. 2004).

If your levels are elevated, you should consider follow-up testing of your B-12, B-6, and folate status:

- B-12: Cobalamin or methylmalonic acid (MMA) test.
- B-6: Blood plasma test for pyriodoxal 5-phosphate (P5P).
- Folate: Red blood cell folate.

Omega-3 Fatty Acids

Most of us do not consume enough Omega-3 fatty acids, so you need to change your diet accordingly. However, if you need to monitor your levels or test your fatty acid metabolism, you can get your blood levels tested at the laboratories listed below.

Minerals

Your doctor can test your status for individual minerals and should certainly test your iron as described below. But there is a blood panel you should consider, if you have the funds (approximately $500), which will measure your levels of various minerals and toxic metals. It is listed below as the "red blood cell panel" in the section on laboratories. It is an all-in-one test and you may have some surprises (arsenic exposure, for example) that can be treated and can alleviate your depression.

Zinc

Serum zinc tests have been used in research (Maes 1994) and should be available from your doctor. But a red blood cell test may be a better measure of your zinc status and is available as part of the red blood cell panel from Doctor's Data, Genova Diagnostics, and Metametrix (see pages 173 and 174). Your doctor may also have access to a red blood cell zinc test.

Iron

Testing for iron deficiency is fairly common. Your doctor should be able to offer you several tests. You will likely start with a hemoglobin test. If that test comes back in the normal range, but you suffer from many of the deficiency signs, ask for a ferritin test as well.

Magnesium

Clinicians generally seem to be frustrated by magnesium testing because typical blood tests often do not indicate a deficiency even when there are other clinical signs of a deficiency and when those signs improve with magnesium supplementation.

Better options still are:

- Red blood cell test (erythrocyte). This test is widely available but the false negative rate is high. It is preferable to serum magnesium.
- A magnesium tolerance test. Magnesium levels measured in urine after a large dose of magnesium has been administered.
- A plasma ionized magnesium test. This test may become more widely available, but it is essentially unavailable at the time of this writing.

Perhaps a better and cheaper alternative is for your doctor to give you a complete medical exam, checking for your magnesium status. Low magnesium is associated with the signs below, which your doctor can check. These are also signs of low calcium. Work with your doctor to determine whether you are low in calcium, magnesium, or both.

Early sign

- Face, hand, and foot numbness and tingling (paresthesias) (Shils 1999, 176)

Severe depletion (from Shills 1999, 176; see also Jong and Rud 2005)

- Positive Chvostek's sign—your facial muscles will twitch when your doctor taps a facial nerve. This is also a sign of low calcium

- Positive Trousseau's sign—the muscles in your wrist or hand will twitch when your doctor has blocked the blood flow to your lower arm (usually with a blood pressure cuff). This too is a sign of low calcium
- Normal or depressed deep tendon reflexes despite low calcium levels
- Spontaneous spasms in your hands (carpopedal spasm)
- Generalized muscle spasms
- Tremors, muscle fasciculations (small involuntary muscle spasms), myoclonic jerks (sudden, involuntary muscle jerks)
- Focal and generalized seizures

Discuss this list and your symptoms with your doctor.

Nutrient Dosage and Toxicity Dangers

Folate

Coppen and Bolander-Gouaille (2005) recommend dietary supplementation of 800 mg/day of folic acid. Consider as well using the methylfolate form of folate. Your body goes through fewer steps to use methylfolate than folic acid. Furthermore, researchers are becoming concerned that unmetabolized folic acid (the folic acid your body does not convert to methylfolate) can actually impair your brain function if you also have a B-12 deficiency (Morris et al. 2007).

B-12

The recommended dose of B-12 is 1 mg/day (Coppen and Bolander-Gouaille 2005). The preferred form of B-12 is methylcobalamin, though it can be difficult to find. See my Web site for current resources.

Vitamin B-6

Vitamin B-6 is a water-soluble vitamin, which means we tend to urinate out any extra that our bodies do not need. However, it can be toxic in high doses. There have been incidences of women using B-6 to self-medicate their premenstrual symptoms who have ended up neurotoxic from high levels of B-6. It is important to remember that you can get too much of a good thing—do not self-medicate in high doses. However, in general, Bernstein (1990) suggests that 100–150 mg per day over a five- to ten-year period is safe. Clinical trials tend to use about 50 mg of B-6 (Doll 1989; DeSouza 2000; Mattes 1982).

Clinicians do use higher doses. Pfeiffer recommends 50 milligrams per day but he used doses of up to 2,000 milligrams per day for people with more severe deficiencies. Some people may need these higher doses, such as those with pyroluria, but people in this category should be working with a doctor as well. So if your doctor puts you on a higher dose, do not be alarmed. He or she probably has good reason. But do not put yourself on too high of a dose. You don't need new problems.

The coenzyme form of B-6, pyriodoxal 5-phosphate (P5P), is a more bioavailable form of vitamin B-6, which simply means that your body will need to go through fewer steps before putting it to use. A common supplement in health food stores, it is more expensive but it is also more effective. The problem is that there is not a clear consensus on P5P dosage. Pfeiffer argues that a milligram of P5P is worth about 10 milligrams of B-6 and would recommend one-tenth the dosage of P5P.

Omega-3 Fatty Acids

Based on the evidence from clinical trials, Andrew Stoll recommends 4 grams of EPA each day for depression. For postpartum depression, he recommends 4 grams of EPA+DHA but he emphasizes the dearth of clinical trials on moms with depression.

Two oils are most commonly recommended as the gold standard for EPA: fish oil and cod liver oil. Cod liver oil has the benefit of having vitamin A and vitamin D, both of which we all need and typically get too little of in our diet. In the winter in particular, with lower sun exposure, people do become vitamin D deficient much easier and are more susceptible to depression.

Whereas the benefit of cod liver oil is the vitamin content, the drawback of cod liver oil is also the vitamin content. When you are taking very high doses of EPA and DHA, you will quickly reach the Dietary Reference Intake (DRI) of vitamin A and D. For this reason, Stoll in *The Omega Connection* recommends using fish oil, devoid of these vitamins. I suggest using both—use a combination of cod liver oil and fish oil each day. Use cod liver oil up to a reasonable level of vitamin A and D (this will require you to think a bit about your diet) and add fish oil on top to finish out the dose of Omega-3 fatty acids that your doctor has recommended.

Minerals

Zinc

Do not take zinc supplements if you have no evidence that you are deficient. Too much zinc can become toxic. The amino chelate forms of zinc tend to be absorbed well. The commonly available form of zinc, zinc oxide, is absorbed least well. Zinc supplements are usually about 40 milligrams per day and some include copper because zinc supplementation can reduce copper absorption (DiSilvestro 2004).

Iron

A low serum ferritin level (15 micrograms per liter and under) suggests low iron. A supplement will be the quickest road to relief. Space your doses through the day to increase your absorption. A dose of about 50 milligrams twice daily is recommended in the case of iron deficiency anemia but you should work with your doctor to adjust your dose for your circumstance. With a less severe deficiency, you may not need as high a dose. If you are not anemic and you take iron supplements, you risk iron toxicity—our bodies excrete very little iron. Children experimenting with parents' iron supplements have died from iron toxicity (Corbett 1995).

Magnesium

Your best long-term strategy is to include magnesium-rich foods in your diet. But a short-term insurance policy for getting out of the depths of muscle twitching and jerking can include a magnesium supplement. Several studies have had good outcomes with 160 milligrams of magnesium citrate (Kuti 1970), though others have used up to 400 milligrams of magnesium lactate (Barthelemy 1980) and 500 milligrams of magnesium aspartate (Abraham 1984), all highly absorbable forms of magnesium.

LABS FOR BLOOD ANALYSIS

Your doctor has access to many labs, but these are some of the more unusual tests that are not generally offered. Your doctor must order all these tests or you can use www.directlabs.com and consult with their doctors on staff.

Red Blood Cell Panel for Mineral Analysis
- Doctor's Data Red Blood Cell Elements. At press time the panel includes thirteen minerals and five toxic metals. Minerals include magnesium, iron, and zinc.
- Genova Diagnostics Element Analysis. At press time the panel includes eight minerals and seven toxic metals. Minerals include magnesium and zinc.
- Metametrix Nutrient Elements. At press time the panel includes nine minerals and five toxic metals. Minerals include magnesium and zinc.

Plasma Homocysteine
- Your local doctor
- Metametrix Plasma Homocysteine

Fatty Acids
- Metametrix Fatty Acids Profile
- Genova Diagnostics Essential and Metabolic Fatty Acids

Amino Acid Profile
- Doctor's Data Plasma Amino Acids

- Genova Diagnostics Amino Acid Analysis (blood)
- Metametrix Bloodspot Amino Acids

Intestinal Balance

- Doctor's Data—extensive selection of tests
- Genova Diagnostics—Comprehensive Digestive Stool Analysis
- Metametrix Organix Dysbiosis

Pyroluria

- Bio-Center Laboratory Pyrroles, biocenterlab.org/

Vitamin D

- Vitamin D, 25-Hydroxy, Metametrix
- Vitamin D, 25-Hydroxy, Life Extension Web site ($63):
  www.lef.org/newshop/items/itemLC081950.html

Lab Contact Information:

Bio-Center Laboratory
3100 North Hillside Avenue
Wichita, KS 67219
316.684.7784
www.brightspot.org/biocenter/

Doctor's Data, Inc.
3755 Illinois Avenue
St. Charles, IL 60174-2420
800.323.2784
www.doctorsdata.com

Genova Diagnostics
63 Zillicoa Street
Asheville, NC 28801
800.522.4762
www.gdx.net

Metametrix Clinical Laboratory
4855 Peachtree Industrial Boulevard, Suite 201
Norcross, GA 30092
800.221.4640
www.metametrix.com

Food Preparation Techniques

Dairy Kefir

There are actually kefir starters available in health food stores that allow you to use a yogurt-like approach to making kefir. This is not the cheapest way to make kefir, nor the traditional approach.

Kefir is cultured from a substance called *kefir grains*. These grains are not anything like what comes to your mind when you hear the word "grain." Kefir grains are a symbiotic mass of bacteria and yeasts that will culture your milk for you. Find kefir grains and follow these instructions.

Milk kefir instructions

1. Put your grains into a clean glass jar. Quart-sized mason jars work well.
2. Cover with about one quart of milk.
3. Place in a cupboard or other spot out of direct sunlight.
4. Cover the jar with a clean dish towel.
5. Let it sit for twenty-four hours or until it reaches desired sourness.
6. When kefir is finished, strain grains from kefir milk.
7. Drink kefir. Reuse grains. Return to step 1.

Kefir don'ts:

- Don't use metal utensils with kefir. To strain the grains you can use a nylon strainer, a plastic slotted spoon, or a plastic colander.
- Don't keep the brewing kefir in the direct sun.
- Don't expose the grains to heat, e.g., don't use a jar right out of a hot dishwasher.

Trouble shooting:

Adjusting to a new home: Your first batch or two of kefir may seem extra yeasty. If that's the case, the kefir is still fine to drink, but your kefir will mellow after the grains have been a week or so in their new home.

Tune-up: Kefir grains take on other strains of bacteria. It is possible for your kefir to seem "off." You may even think you killed your grains. You probably didn't. Rinse them with filtered water (nonchlorinated), put them in a glass container, cover with filtered water, and store in the refrigerator for twenty-four hours. Strain them and make a new batch of kefir. Consider it a "tune up."

Storing grains: If you want to take a break from your kefir making for a while, put the grains in a jar with milk (as you would to make kefir), cover with a tight-fitting lid (a canning lid with plastic wrap between the lid and the glass would suffice), and store in the refrigerator. The low temperature will slow down the fermentation process of the grains; they will go into a semi-dormant state. Every week or two, change the milk and drink the kefir that you made in your refrigerator. Your grains may last longer than this, so if you do neglect them for a time, try to rejuvenate them before deciding you have killed them. Make a batch or two of kefir and see how they do.

Kefir Sodas
To make kefir sodas, you can use a commercial kefir starter available at some health food stores, or choose a cheaper path and acquire water kefir grains. These grains are a different strain than the milk kefir grains and will create a fizzy soda-like drink. I cannot recommend this drink highly enough.

Water kefir instructions
1. Dissolve ⅓ of a cup of sugar with warm water in a clean glass jar.
2. Add one quart of filtered water. Do not use municipal chlorinated water. It will affect your grains adversely.
3. Add grains.
4. Place in a cupboard or other spot out of direct sunlight.
5. Cover the jar with a clean dish towel.
6. Let it sit for twenty-four hours.
7. Strain grains from liquid.
8. Add 1 cup of juice, the juice of one lemon, or any other fruit concoction.
9. Let liquid brew until it reaches desired sweetness. Strain the grains. Return to step 1.

Water kefir don'ts:
- Don't use metal utensils with kefir. To strain the grains you can use a nylon strainer, a plastic slotted spoon, or a plastic colander.
- Don't keep brewing kefir in the direct sun.
- Don't expose the grains to heat, e.g., don't use a jar right out of a hot dishwasher. Don't add grains to the hot water used to dissolve sugar.

Storing grains. If you want to take a break from your kefir making for a while, put the grains in a jar with sugar water (as you would to make kefir), cover with a tight-fitting lid (a canning lid with plastic wrap between the lid and the glass would suffice), and store in the refrigerator. The low temperature will slow down the fermentation process of the grains; they will go into a semi-dormant state. Every week or two, change the sugar water and make a kefir beverage from the water that was fermented in your refrigerator. Your grains may last longer than this, so if you do neglect them for a time, try to rejuvenate them before deciding you have killed them. Make a batch or two of kefir soda and see how they do.

Type of sugar. You can use refined or unrefined sugar for your kefir. The biggest difference will be cost and mineral content. White refined sugar is cheap but it has no mineral content. Unrefined cane sugar is reasonably priced if you can find it in bulk. It will add minerals to your drink, particularly magnesium.

Yogurt

Yogurt is a traditional method of preserving milk that adds beneficial bacteria to the milk product. The process is fairly simple: heat the milk to scalding to kill competing bacteria, cool the milk to about 110°F, add a bacteria starter, and keep the milk at 110°F for twenty-four hours.

Supplies:
1. Starter. Use about a ¼ cup portion of a live culture yogurt for every quart of milk. Warm to body temperature, or about 100°F. Alternatively, buy a yogurt starter, a more foolproof method.
2. Stainless steel bowl or pot to heat milk. (See double-boiler method below.)
3. Container to culture yogurt. This can be a glass mason jar or the container that comes with a yogurt maker.
4. Optional: digital thermometer with alarm. (Alarm sounds when the heating milk reaches the desired temperature.)

Heating milk, adding starter:
1. Use a double-boiler method to scald milk. I put the milk in a large stainless steel bowl and set the bowl in a sauté pan filled with water.
2. Set a timer so that you remember to check the milk as it cooks on the stove. Alternatively, use a digital thermometer with an alarm set at 180°F.
3. Pull the milk off the heat just before it boils.
4. Set the milk on the counter in an out-of-the-way place and set your digital thermometer 110°F. Without a digital thermometer, check the milk every twenty minutes (set a kitchen timer to remind you). It is ready when it is just above body temperature. Do not stick your finger in to check the temperature. Take a small amount out with a spoon and drip it onto the back of your hand. When it is no longer hot to the touch, it is ready for starter.
5. Have all your containers ready so that when your milk is ready for the starter, you do not have to go into a frenzy.

6. When the milk cools, add some to a smaller bowl or cup. Add the starter to this smaller container. Mix it in well. Add the mixture to the main bowl. Mix well.

7. Pour the milk with the starter mixture into the yogurt containers.

8. Set in a warm location for twenty-four hours. This is the step where people find a yogurt maker to be handy. Yogurt makers will maintain a temperature of 110°F. I used the Yogourmet yogurt maker because I could make a half gallon at a time and it would hold its heat for as long as I wanted to culture the milk. I have given the yogurt maker away, however, because I make one gallon at a time now. A yogurt maker is convenient for smaller quantities, but it is not necessary.

The key is to keep your milk at about 110°F. The yogurt will be forgiving, however. Some of the more common methods include the following:

1. **Cooler.** Put your jars of milk in a cooler, in a few inches of warm water. The water helps maintain a warm environment in the cooler for the twenty-four hours. In the summer I put the cooler in a sunny part of the house with a blanket over it to regulate the temperature over the whole cooler. In the winter I put the cooler near a woodstove with a blanket over it. In the winter I also change the water at least once in the twenty-four hours to keep the warm environment in the cooler. A cooler too close to the woodstove is a bad idea. This is where trial and error will help find the right spot.

2. **Oven.** If you have an oven with a pilot or an oven light that maintains a warm environment, this might be a good location for your jars. A warming drawer could also work.

3. **Heating pad.** Experiment by keeping your yogurt warm on a heating pad.

Raw milk yogurt
Follow the recipe above, but heat the milk to 110°F. Once milk hits 110°F, add starter and keep warm per the instructions above.

Note that raw milk yogurt does not tend to congeal as well as pasteurized yogurt. Expect something more like a yogurt drink.

Fermented vegetables
Home fermentation is very simple and satisfying, but there are some methods and tools you will need.

Supplies:

1. Crock. At yard sales keep an eye out for antique pickle crocks. You can also buy some very nice crocks online if it is in your budget.
2. Weight. You will need a plate a bit smaller than the opening of your crock to fit on top of your vegetables. Depending on the plate, you will likely need a weight on top of the plate.
3. Salt.
4. Vegetables.

Instructions:

1. Clean your crock, plate, and weight well.
2. Chop up your vegetables to your desired size.
3. Put a 2-inch layer of vegetables in your crock.
4. Pound them and swish them with your clean fists.
5. Sprinkle a teaspoon or so of salt onto the vegetable layer.
6. Continue to layer, pound, and salt until the crock is about three-quarters full.
7. Fill the crock with water until the water is a couple of inches from the top.
8. Set the clean plate on the vegetables. Make sure all vegetables are under the water.
9. Add the weight on top of the plate to keep the plate and vegetables securely under water. A boiled rock works well as a weight.
10. Cover with a dish towel. Let the vegetables ferment for a week or longer. Sample as you wish.
11. When done, you may store your creation in the refrigerator.

Fermented squash and peppers taste great on a salad or as a small side dish in a heavy meal. Visit my Web site for more ideas or purchase Sandor Katz's *Wild Fermentation* to get started.

Sourdough

Sourdough starter is simply flour and water inhabited by airborne yeast. The starter is used in bread as a rising agent. It adds flavor and zest to cakes and crusts. And it is a natural phytate-reducer. If you have not tried making your own sourdough, you should start with the pancakes. You will never turn back.

Traditional starter

For a traditional starter you will make a batter and capture yeasts from the air to bring it to life. In a scalded bowl to kill bacteria, add 2 cups of flour and enough body temperature water to make a thick batter. Cover the bowl with a towel and let it sit in a warm place for about five days. When it begins to bubble, it will be ready for pancakes. Remove half of the starter for your sourdough recipe and add a new cup of flour and some water to the bowl. Let it sit until it bubbles. Make more sourdough.

You can purchase sourdough starters online or get a starter from a friend who makes sourdough. It is difficult for beginners to get a starter started, so you might want to use the cheater's method below while you try to acquire someone else's starter.

Cheater's starter

If the traditional starter scares you, if you do not want to purchase one, or you just forgot to get it started, this is for you. With this approach you do not use yeast in the air to raise your dough, you combine equal parts warm water and flour and add about a tablespoon of baker's yeast for every 2 cups of flour. Mix thoroughly and let sit until it rises. It will rise in just a few hours in warm weather.

Pancake recipe

The night before the pancake breakfast, mix your starter and an additional 2 cups of flour with enough warm water to make a batter. If you used the cheater's starter method, simply make about 3 cups of cheater's starter the night before. This whole process is very forgiving so do not worry too much about exact amounts of flour. In the morning, stir the batter a bit (but do not stir too much or you will lose some of the lightness in the batter), heat up your griddle, and add the following ingredients to the batter:

> 2 eggs beaten
> ⅓ cup melted coconut oil or butter
> 2 tsp salt
> Optional: up to five egg whites for added protein and fluffy pancakes

> Mix the ingredients into batter gently. Heat about ¼ cup of water and mix with 1 tsp baking soda. Add the dissolved baking soda to the batter just before cooking pancakes. Coconut oil is my preferred oil for cooking the occasional pancake.

Internet Resources:

www.sourdo.com
home.att.net/~carlsfriends
www.sourdoughhome.com

Germination

Use raw nuts, seeds, and legumes. Make sure they are untreated. Store them in an airtight container to keep bugs out. Fresher foods will germinate better.

Germination steps

1. Measure the amount of nuts, seeds, or legumes you wish to germinate.
2. Rinse them well.
3. Put them in bowl, cover them with water, and let them soak overnight.
4. Rinse them well in the morning.
5. Place yours seeds in glass jar, cover the jar with cheesecloth, and secure the cheesecloth with a rubber band. Place the jar tilted on a plate to allow for drainage.
6. Rinse your sprouts daily.
7. Sprout to taste. A longer germination will increase the vitamin content. For nuts that you want to keep whole, sprout them for two days or until a small tail begins to form.
8. Rinse your sprouts when ready. Store them in the refrigerator.

Drying step

If you are producing a whole nut or seed as a snack but want to sprout it to reduce phytates and increase the nutrient content, rinse the sprouted nut or seed and place on a cookie sheet. Place in a warm oven (100°F is optimal to preserve the enzymes) or in the sun (cover with a screen or sheer cloth to keep the birds out).

References

Abou-Fadel, O.S. and L.T. Miller. 1983. "Vitamin retention, colour, and texture in thermally processed green beans and Royal Ann cherries packed in pouches and cans." *Journal of Food Science* 48(3):920–3.

Adams, P.W., D.P. Rose, J. Folkard, V. Wynn, M. Seed, and R. Strong. 1973. "Effect of pyridoxine hydrochloride (vitamin B-6) upon depression associated with oral contraception." *Lancet* 7809(1):899–904.

Alessandri, J.M., P. Guesnet, S. Vancassel, P. Astorg, I. Denis, B. Langelier, S. Aid, C. Poumes-Ballihaut, G. Champeil-Potokar, and M. Lavialle. 2004. "Polyunsaturated fatty acids in the central nervous system: evolution of concepts and nutritional implications throughout life." *Reproduction, Nutrition, Development* 44(6):509–38.

Babu, S. 1976. "Effect of germination on folic acid content of Bengalgram and ragi." *Indian Journal of Nutrition and Dietetics* 13(5):139–41.

Banki, C.M. 1985. "Biochemical markers for suicidal behavior." *American Journal of Psychiatry* 42(1):147–8.

Bargo, F., J.E. Delahoy, G.F. Schroeder, and L.D. Muller, 2006. "Milk fatty acid composition of dairy cows grazing at two pasture allowances and supplemented with different levels and sources of concentrate." *Animal Feed Science and Technology* 24(1–2):17–31.

Beard, J.L., M.K. Hendricks, E.M. Perez, L.E. Murray-Kolb, A. Berg, L. Vernon-Feagans, J. Irlam, W. Isaacs, A. Sive, and M. Tomlinson. 2005. "Maternal iron deficiency anemia affects postpartum emotions and cognition." *Journal of Nutrition* 135(2):267–72.

Bedogni, G. and N.C. Battistini. 2002. "Effects of cooking and storage on the nutritional value of eggs." R.R. Watson, ed., *Eggs in Health Promotion*. Ames: Iowa State Press.

Bell, I.R., J.S. Edman, F.D. Morrow, D.W. Marby, G. Perrone, H.L. Kayne, M. Greenwald, J.O. Cole. 1992. "Brief communication. Vitamin B1, B2, and B6 augmentation of tricyclic antidepressant treatment in geriatric depression with cognitive dysfunction." *Journal of the American College of Nutrition* 11(2):159–63.

Bergqvist, S.W., A.S. Sandberg, N.G. Carlsson, T. Andlid, 2005. "Improved iron solubility in carrot juice fermented by homo- and hetero-fermentative lactic acid bacteria." *Food Microbiology* 22(1):53–61.

Bernstein, A.L., 1990. "Vitamin B6 in clinical neurology." *Annals of the New York Academy of Sciences* 585(1):250–60.

Bohn, T., L. Davidsson, T. Walczyk, and R. Hurrell. 2004. "Phytic acid added to white wheat bread inhibits fractional apparent magnesium absorption in humans." *Journal of Clinical Nutrition* 79(3):418–23.

Bohn, T., L. Davidsson, T. Walczyk, and R.F. Hurrell. 2004. "Fractional magnesium absorption is significantly lower in human subjects from a meal served with an oxalate-rich vegetable, spinach, as compared with a meal served with kale, a vegetable with a low oxalate content." *British Journal of Nutrition* 91(4):601–06.

Bolourchi-Vaghefi, S. 2002. "Eggs and health: Myths and misconceptions." R.R. Watson, ed., *Eggs in Health Promotion*. Ames: Iowa State Press.

Bottiglieri, T., M. Laundry, R. Crellin, B.K. Toone, M.W. Carney, and E.H. Reynolds. 2000. "Homocysteine, folate, methylation, and monoamine metabolism in depression." *Journal of Neurology, Neurosurgery, and Psychiatry* 69(2):228–32.

Breslow, J.L. 2006. "n-3 Fatty acids and cardiovascular disease." *American Journal of Clinical Nutrition* 83:S1477–82.

Brzezinski, E., A.M. Durning, B. Grasse, Fusselman, T. Ciaraldi. 1998. "Oxalate content of selected foods." San Diego: University of California.

Catargi, B. F. Parrot-Roulaud, C. Cochet, D. Ducassou, P. Roger, and A. Tabarin. 1999. "Homocysteine, hypothyroidism, and effect of thyroid hormone replacement." *Thyroid* 9(12):1163–6.

Chai, W. and M. Liebman. 2005. "Effect of different cooking methods on vegetable oxalate content." *Journal of Agriculture and Food Chemistry* 53(8):3027–30.

Cherian, G. and J.S. Sim. 1996. "Changes in the breast milk fatty acids and plasma lipids of nursing mothers following consumption of n-3 polyunsaturated fatty acid enriched eggs." *Nutrition* 12(1):8–12.

Coppen, A. and J. Bailey. 2000. "Enhancement of the antidepressant action of fluoxetine by folic acid: A randomised, placebo controlled trial." *Journal of Affective Disorders* 60(2):121–30.

Coppen, A. and C. Bolander-Gouaille. 2005. "Treatment of depression: time to consider folic acid and vitamin B12." *Journal of Psychopharmacology* 19(1):59–65.

Corapci, F., A.E. Radan, B. Lozoff. 2006. "Iron deficiency in infancy and mother-child interaction at 5 years." *Journal of Developmental and Behavioral Pediatrics* 27(5):371–8.

Corbett, J.V. 1995. "Accidental poisoning with iron supplements." *American Journal of Maternal Child Nursing* 20(4):234.

Corwin, E.J., L.E. Murray-Kolb, and J.L. Beard, 2003. "Low hemoglobin level is a risk factor for postpartum depression." *Journal of Nutrition* 133(12):4139–42.

Couvreur, S., C. Hurtaud, C. Lopez, L. Delaby, and J.L. Peyraud. 2006. "The linear relationship between the proportion of fresh grass in the cow diet, milk fatty acid composition, and butter properties." *Journal of Dairy Science* 89(6):1956–69.

Cox, I.M., M.J. Campbell, and D. Dowson. 1991. "Red blood cell magnesium and chronic fatigue syndrome." *Lancet* 337(8744):757–60.

Cross-National Collaborative Group. 1992. "The changing rate of major depression. Cross-national comparisons." *Journal of the American Medical Association* 268(21):3098–3105.

Czerniejewski, C.P., C.W. Shank, W.G. Bechtel, and W.B. Bradley. 1964. "The minerals of wheat, flour and bread." *Cereal Chemistry* 41(2):65–72.

Davis, D. R., M.D. Epp, and H.D. Riordan. 2004. "Changes in USDA food composition data for 43 garden crops, 1950 to 1999." *Journal of the American College of Nutrition* 23:669–82.

Dean, Carolyn. 2004. *The Miracle of Magnesium*. New York: Simon & Schuster Ltd.

de Groot, R.H., G. Hornstra, A.C. van Houwelingen, and F. Roumen, 2004. "Effect of alpha-linolenic acid supplementation during pregnancy on maternal and neonatal polyunsaturated fatty acid status and pregnancy outcome." *American Journal of Clinical Nutrition* 79(2):251–60.

Demirel, G., H. Ozpinar, B. Nazli, and O Keser. 2006. "Fatty acids of lamb meat from two breeds fed different forage: concentrate ratio." *Meat Science* 72(2):229–35.

Denomme, J., K.D. Stark, and B.J. Holub. 2005. "Directly quantitated dietary (n-3) fatty acid intakes of pregnant canadian women are lower than current dietary recommendations." *Journal of Nutrition* 135(2):206–11.

De Souza, M.C., A.F. Walker, P.A. Robinson, and K. Bolland. 2000. "A synergistic effect of a daily supplement for 1 month of 200 mg magnesium plus 50 mg vitamin B6 for the relief of anxiety-related premenstrual symptoms: A randomized, double-blind, crossover study." *Journal of Women's Health and Gender-Based Medicine* 9(2):131–39.

Dhiman, T.R., G.R. Anand, L.D. Satter, and M.W. Pariza. 1999. "Conjugated linoleic acid content of milk from cows fed different diets." *Journal of Dairy Science* 82(10):2146–56.

Disilvestro, Robert A. 2004. *Handbook of Minerals as Nutritional Supplements*. Boca Raton: CRC Press.

Doll, H., S. Brown, A. Thurston, and M. Vessey. 1989. "Pyridoxine (vitamin B6) and the premenstrual syndrome: a randomized crossover trial." *Journal of the Royal College of General Practitioners* 39(326):364–68.

Duckett, S.K., D.G. Wagner, L.D. Yates, H.G. Dolezal, and S.G. May. 1993. "Effects of time on feed on beef nutrient composition." *Journal of Animal Science* 71(8):2079–88.

Duke, James A. 1992. *Handbook of phytochemical constituents of GRAS herbs and other economic plants*. Boca Raton: CRC Press.

Ebbesson, S.O., L.O. Ebbesson, M. Swenson, J.M. Kennish, and D.C. Robbins, 2005. "A successful diabetes prevention study in Eskimos: The Alaska Siberia project." *International Journal of Circumpolar Health* 64(4):409–24.

Egli, I., L. Davidsson, M.A. Juillierat, D. Barclay, and R. Hurrell. 2003. "Phytic acid degradation in complementary foods using phytase naturally occurring in whole grain cereals." *Journal of Food Science* 68(5):1855–9.

Egli, I., L. Davidsson, and C. Zeder. 2004. "Dephitinization of complementary foods based on wheat and soy increased zinc, but not copper, apparent absorption in adults." *Journal of Nutrition* 134(5):1077–80.

Egounlety, M. and O.C. Aworth. 2003. "Effect of soaking, dehulling, cooking and fermentation with Rhizopus oligosporus on the oligosaccharides, trypsin inhibitor, phytic acid and tannins of soybean (*Glycine max Merr.*), cowpea (*Vigna unguiculata L. Walp*) and groundbean (*Macrotyloma geocarpa Harms*)." *Journal of Food Engineering* 56(2/3):249–54.

Enser, M., K.G. Hallett, B. Hewett, G.A.J. Fursey, J.D. Wood, and G. Harrington. 1998. "Fatty acid content and composition of UK beef and lamb muscle in relation to production system and implications for human nutrition." *Meat Science* 49(3):329–41.

Environmental Protection Agency. Uranium Fact Sheet. http://www.epa.gov/radiation/radionuclides/uranium.htm (accessed May 2006).

Fava M., J.S. Borus, J.E. Alpert, A.A. Nierenberg, J.F. Rosenbaum, and T. Bottiglieri, 1997. "Folate, vitamin B12, and homocysteine in major depressive disorder." *American Journal of Psychiatry* 154(3):426–8.

Foran, J.A., D.H. Good, D.O. Carpenter, M.C. Hamilton, B.A. Knuth, and S.J. Schwager. 2005. "Quantitative analysis of the benefits and risks of consuming farmed and wild salmon." *Journal of Nutrition* 135(11):2639–43.

Francois C.A., S.L. Connor, L.C. Bolewicz, and W.E. Connor. 2003. "Supplementing lactating women with flaxseed oil does not increase docosahexaenoic acid in their milk." *American Journal of Clinical Nutrition* 77(1):226–33.

Godfrey P.S., B.K. Toone, M.W. Carney, T.G. Flynn, T. Bottiglieri, M. Laundy, I. Chanarin, and E.H. Reynolds. 1990. "Enhancement of recovery from psychiatric illness by methylfolate." *Lancet* 336(8712):392–5.

Goldenberg R.L., T. Tamura, Y. Neggers, R.L. Copper, K.E. Johnston, M.B. DuBard, and J.C. Hauth. 1995. "The effect of zinc supplementation on pregnancy outcome." *Journal of the American Medical Association* 274(6):463–8.

Harland, B.F. and D. Oberleas. 1987. "Phytate in Foods." *World Review of Nutrition and Dietetics* 52:235–59.

Harper, C.R., M.J. Edwards, A.P. DeFilipis, and T.A. Jacobson. 2006. "Flaxseed Oil Increases the Plasma Concentrations of Cardioprotective (n-3) Fatty Acids in Humans." *Journal of Nutrition* 136(1):83–87.

Hebeisen, D.F., F. Hoeflin, H.P. Reusch, E. Junker, and B.H. Lauterburg. 1993. "Increased concentrations of omega-3 fatty acids in milk and platelet rich plasma of grass-fed cows." *International Journal for Vitamin and Nutrition Research* 63(3):229–33.

Heller, S., R.M. Salkeld, and W.F. Körner. 1973. "Vitamin B6 status in pregnancy." *American Journal of Clinical Nutrition* 26(12):1339–48.

Herbert, V. 1987. "Recommended dietary intakes (RDI) of vitamin B-12 in humans." *American Journal of Clinical Nutrition* 45(4):671–8.

Herbert, V. 1988. "Vitamin B-12: Plant Sources, Requirements, and Assay." *American Journal of Clinical Nutrition* 48(3):852–8.

Hibbeln, J.R. 2002. "Seafood consumption, the DHA content of mothers' milk and prevalence rates of postpartum depression: A cross-national, ecological analysis." *Journal of Affective Disorders* 69(1–3):15–29.

Hodgkinson, A. 1977. *Oxalic Acid Biology and Medicine*. New York: Academic Press.

Hoffman, R., E. Benz, S. Shattil, B. Furie, H. Cohen, L. Silberstein, and P. McGlave. 2000. *Hematology: Basic Principles and Practice*, 3rd ed. Ch 26: "Disorders of iron metabolism: Iron deficiency and overload." New York: Churchill Livingstone, Harcourt Brace & Co.

Huan, M., K. Hamazaki, Y. Sun, M. Itomura, H. Liu, W. Kang, S. Watanabe, K. Terasawa, and T. Hamazaki. 2004. "Suicide attempt and n-3 fatty acid levels in red blood cells: A case control study in China." *Biological Psychiatry* 56(7):490–496.

Huang, Zhi-Bin, H. Leibovitz, C.M Lee, and R. Millar. 1990. "Effect of dietary fish oil on n-3 fatty acid levels in chicken eggs and thigh flesh." *Journal of Agricultural and Food Chemistry* 38(3):743–47.

Hurrell, R.F., M. B. Reddy, M.-A Juillerat and J. D. Cook. 2003. "Degradation of phytic acid in cereal porridges improves iron absorption by human subjects." *American Journal of Clinical Nutrition* 77(5):1213–9.

Hvas A.M., S. Juul, P. Bech, and E. Nexo. 2004. "Vitamin B6 level is associated with symptoms of depression." *Psychotherapy Psychosomatics* 73(6):340–3.

Innis, S.M. and S. L. Elias, 2003. "Intakes of essential n-6 and n-3 polyunsaturated fatty acids among pregnant Canadian women." *American Journal of Clinical Nutrition* 77(2):473–8.

Jong, G.M. and R.K. Rud, 2005. "Magnesium deficiency in critical illness." *Journal of Intensive Care Medicine* 20(15):3.

Katz, Sandor Ellix. 2003. *Wild Fermentation: The Flavor, Nutrition, and Craft of Live-Culture Foods*. White River Junction: Chelsea Green.

Keen, C.L. and L.S. Hurley. 1989. "Zinc and reproduction: Effects of deficiency on foetal and postnatal development," Mills C.F. ed. *Zinc in Human Biology*. New York: Springer-Verlag.

Kendler, K.S., A. Heath, N.G. Martin, and L.J. Eaves. 1986. "Symptoms of anxiety and depression in a volunteer twin population: The etiologic role of genetic and environmental factors." *Archives of General Psychiatry* 43(3):213–21.

Kouba, M., M. Enser, F.M. Whittington, G.R. Nute, and J.D. Wood. 2003. "Effect of a high-linolenic acid diet on lipogenic enzyme activities, fatty acid composition, and meat quality in the growing pig." *Journal of Animal Science* 81(8):1967–79.

Kronberg, S.L., G. Barceló-Coblijn, J. Shin, K. Lee, and E.J. Murphy. 2006. "Bovine muscle n-3 fatty acid content is increased with flaxseed feeding." *Lipids* 41(11):1059–68.

Lerner, V., C. Miodownik, A. Kaptsan, H. Cohen, U. Loewenthal, and M. Kotler. 2002. "Vitamin B6 as add-on treatment in chronic schizophrenic and schizoaffective patients: A double-blind, placebo-controlled study." *Journal of Clinical Psychiatry* 63(1):54–8.

Lipski, Elizabeth. 2004. *Digestive Wellness*. New York: McGraw-Hill.

Llorente A.M., C.L. Jensen, R.G. Voigt, J.K. Fraley, M.C. Berretta, and W.C. Heird. 2003. "Effect of maternal docosahexaenoic acid supplementation on postpartum depression and information processing." *American Journal of Obstetrics and Gynecology* 188(5):1348–1353.

Lopez-Alonso M., Bendito J.L., Miranda M., Castillo C., Hernandez J., and Shore R.F. 2000. "Toxic and trace elements in liver, kidney and meat from cattle slaughtered in Galicia (NW Spain)." *Food Additives and Contaminants* 17(6):447–57.

Maes, M., P.C. D'Haese, S. Scharpe, P. D'Hondt, P. Cosyns, and M.E. De Broe. 1994. "Hypozincemia in depression." *Journal of Affective Disorders* 31(2):135–40.

Marangell, L.B., J.M. Martinez, H.A. Zboyan, H. Chong., and L.J. Puryear. 2004. "Omega-3 fatty acids for the prevention of postpartum depression: Negative data from a preliminary, open-label pilot study." *Depression and Anxiety* 19(1):20–23.

Martner-Hewes, P.M., I.F. Hunt, N.J. Murphy, M.E. Swendseid, R.H. and Settlage R.H. 1986. "Vitamin B-6 nutriture and plasma diamine oxidase activity in pregnant Hispanic teenagers." *American Journal of Clinical Nutrition* 44(6):907–13.

Marier, J.R. 1986. "Magnesium content of the food supply in the modern-day world." *Magnesium* 5(1):1–8.

Mattes, J.A. and D. Martin, 1982. "Pyridoxine in premenstrual depression." *Human Nutrition Applied Nutrition* 36(2):131–3.

McCance, R.A., 1978. *McCance and Widdowson's The Composition of Foods*. Elsevier/North Holland Biomedical Press.

Mellanby, Edward, Sir. 1950. *A Story of Nutritional Research*. Baltimore: Williams and Wilkins.

Mezzacappa, E.S. and E.S. Katkin. 2002. "Breast-feeding is associated with reduced perceived stress and negative mood in mothers." *Health Psychology* 21(2):187–93.

Morris, M.S, P.F. Jacques, I.H. Rosenberg, and J. Selhub. 2007. "Folate and vitamin B-12 status in relation to anemia, macrocytosis, and cognitive impairment in older Americans in the age of folic acid fortification." *American Journal of Clinical Nutrition* 85(1):193–200.

Muriel, E., J. Ruiz, J. Ventanas and T. Antequera. 2002. "Free-range rearing increases (n-3) polyunsaturated fatty acids of neutral and polar lipids in swine muscles." *Food Chemistry* 78(2):219–25.

Naito, Y., T. Nagata, Y. Takano, T. Nagatsu and N. Ohara. 2003. "Rapeseed oil ingestion and exacerbation of hypertension-related conditions in stroke prone spontaneously hypertensive rats." *Toxicology* 187(2-3):205–16.

Nemets, B., Z. Stahl, and R.H. Belmaker. 2002. "Addition of Omega-3 Fatty Acid to Maintenance Medication Treatment for Recurrent Unipolar Depressive Disorder." *American Journal of Psychiatry* 159(3):477–9.

Nowak, G., M. Siwek, D. Dudek, A. Zieba, and A. Pilc. 2003. "Effect of zinc supplementation on antidepressant therapy in unipolar depression: A preliminary placebo-controlled study." *Polish Journal of Pharmacology* 55(6):1143–7.

Nowak, G., Szewczyk B., and Pilc A. 2005. "Zinc and depression: An update." *Pharmacological Reports* 57(6):713–8.

Oberleas D. and B.F. Harland. 1981. "Phytate content of foods: effect on dietary zinc bioavailability." *Journal of American Dietetic Association* 79(4):433–6.

Ohara, N., Y. Naito, T. Nagata, K. Tatematsu, S.Y. Fuma, S. Tachibana, and H. Okuyama. 2006. "Exploration for unknown substances in rapeseed oil that shorten survival time of stroke-prone spontaneously hypertensive rats: Effects of super critical gas extraction fractions." *Food and Chemical Toxicology* 44(7):952–63.

Papazachariou, I.M., A. Martinez-Isla, E. Efthimiou, R.C. Williamson, and S.I. Girgis. 2000. "Magnesium deficiency in patients with chronic pancreatitis identified by an intravenous loading test." *Clinica Chimica Acta* 302(1-2):145–54.

Peet, M. and D.F. Horrobin. 2002. "A dose-ranging study of the effects of ethyl-eicosapentaenoate in patients with ongoing depression despite apparently adequate treatment with standard drugs." *Archives of General Psychiatry* 59(10):913–919.

Penninx, B.W., G. M. Guralnik, L. Ferrucci, L. P. Fried, R.H. Allen, and S.P. Stabler. 2000. "Vitamin B12 deficiency and depression in physically disabled older women: Epidemiologic evidence from the Women's Health and Aging Study." *American Journal of Psychiatry* 157(5):715–21.

Price, W. A. 2004 (reprint). *Nutrition and Physical Degeneration.* San Diego: Price-Pottenger Nutrition Foundation.

Procter A. 1991. "Enhancement of recovery from psychiatric illness by methylfolate." *British Journal of Psychiatry.* 159:271–2.

Rasic, J.L. 1987. "Nutritive value of yogurt." *Cultured Dairy Products Journal.* 22(3):6–9.

Reddy, N.R., M.D. Pierson, S.K. Sathe, D.K. Salunkhe, 1989. *Phytates in Cereals and Legumes.* Boca Raton: CRC Press.

Refsum, H., A.D. Smith, P.M. Ueland, E. Nexo, R. Clarke, J. McPartlin, C. Johnston, F. Engbaek, J. Schneede, C. McPartlin, and J.M. Scott. 2004. "Facts and Recommendations about Total Homocysteine Determinations: An Expert Opinion." *Clinical Chemistry* 50(1):3–32.

Reiterer G., R. Macdonald, J.D. Browning, J. Morrow, S.V. Matveev, A. Daugherty, E. Smart, M. Toborek, and B. Hennig. 2005. "Zinc Deficiency Increases Plasma Lipids and Atherosclerotic Markers in LDL-Receptor-Deficient Mice." *Journal of Nutrition* 135(9):2114–8.

Rogers, Sherry A. 1997. *Depression Cured at Last!* Syracuse: Prestige Publishing.

Scholl, T.O., M.L. Hediger, J.I. Schall, R.L. Fischer, and C.S. Khoo, 1993. "Low zinc intake during pregnancy: its association with preterm and very preterm delivery." *American Journal of Epidemiology* 137(10):1115–24.

Schuster, K., L.B. Bailey, and C.S. Mahan. 1981. "Vitamin B6 status of low-income adolescent and adult pregnant women and the condition of their infants at birth." *American Journal of Clinical Nutrition* 34(9):1731–5.

Schroeder, G.F., J.J. Couderc, F. Bargo, and D.H. Rearte. 2005. "Milk production and fatty acid profile of milk fat by dairy cows fed a winter oats (*Avena sativa* L.) pasture only or a total mixed ration." *New Zealand Journal of Agricultural Research* 48(1):187–95.

Schroeder, H.A. 1971. "Losses of vitamins and trace minerals resulting from processing and preservation of foods." *American Journal of Clinical Nutrition* 24(5):562–73.

Shils, M.E., J.A. Olson, M. Shike, A.C. Ross, eds. 1999. *Modern Nutrition in Health and Disease.* New York: Lippincott Williams & Wilkins; 9th edition.

Simopoulos, A.P. and N. Salem, 1989. "n-3 fatty acids in eggs from range-fed Greek chickens." *New England Journal of Medicine.* 321(20):1412.

Simopoulos A.P., 2002. "Omega-3 fatty acids in inflammation and autoimmune diseases." *Journal of the American College of Nutrition* 21(6):495-505.

Singewald, N., C. Sinner, A. Hetzenauer, S.B. Sartori and H. Murck. "Magnesium-deficient diet alters depression- and anxiety-related behavior in mice—influence of desipramine and Hypericum perforatum extract." *Neuropharmacology* 47(8):1189-97.

Smith, B.L. 1993. "Organic foods vs. supermarket foods: Element levels." *Journal of Applied Nutrition* 45(1):35-39.

Starobrat-Hermelin, B. and T. Kozielec. 1997. "The effects of magnesium physiological supplementation on hyperactivity in children with attention deficit hyperactivity disorder (ADHD). Positive response to magnesium oral loading test." *Magnesium Research* 10(2):149-56.

Stoll A.L., W.E. Severus, M.P. Freeman, S. Rueter, H.A. Zboyan, E. Diamond, K.K. Cress, and L.B. Marangell. 1999. "Omega 3 Fatty Acids in Bipolar Disorder: A Preliminary Double-blind, Placebo-Controlled Trial." *Archives of General Psychiatry* 56(5):407-12.

Stoll, Andrew. 2002. *The Omega-3 Connection: The Groundbreaking Antidepression Diet and Brain Program.* New York: Simon and Schuster.

Su, K.P., S-Y Huang, C-C Chiu, and W.W. Shen. 2003. "Omega-3 fatty acids in major depressive disorder: A preliminary double-blind, placebo-controlled trial." *European Neuropsychopharmacology* 13(4):267-71.

Sutardi and K.A. Buckle. 1985. "Reduction in Phytic Acid Levels in Soybeans During Tempeh Production, Storage and Frying." *Journal of Food Science* 50(1):260-63.

Takenaka S., S. Sugiyama, S. Ebara, E. Miyamoto, K. Abe, Y. Tamura, F. Watanabe, S. Tsuyama, and Y. Nakano. 2001. "Feeding dried purple laver (nori) to vitamin B12-deficient rats significantly improves vitamin B12 status." *British Journal of Nutrition* 85(6):699-703.

Tiemeier, H., H. Ruud van Tuijl, A. Hofman, A. J Kiliaan, and M. Breteler. 2003. "Plasma fatty acid composition and depression are associated in the elderly: the Rotterdam Study." *American Journal of Clinical Nutrition* 78(1):40-6.

United States Department of Agriculture, 1984. "Oxalic Acid Content of Selected Vegetables." http://www.nal.usda.gov/fnic/foodcomp/Data/Other/oxalic.html (accessed May 2006).

Vallee, B.L. and K.H. Falchuk. 1993. "The biochemical basis of zinc physiology." *Physiological Reviews* 73(1):79-118.

Van Loo J., J. Cummings, N. Delzenne, H. Englyst, A. Franck, M. Hopkins, N. Kok, G. Macfarlane, D. Newton, M. Quigley, M. Roberfroid, T. van Vliet, and E. van den Heuvel. 1999. "Functional food properties of non-digestible oligosaccharides: A consensus report from the ENDO project (DGXII AIRII-CT94-1095)." *British Journal of Nutrition* 81(2):121-32.

Vollset S.E., H. Refsum, L.M. Irgens, B.M. Emblem, A. Tverdal, H.K. Gjessing, A.L. Monsen, and P.M. Ueland. 2000. "Plasma total homocysteine, pregnancy complications, and adverse pregnancy outcomes: The Hordaland Homocysteine study." *American Journal of Clinical Nutrition* 71(4):962-8.

Walker, A.F., G. Marakis, S. Christie, and M. Byng. 2003. "Mg citrate found more bioavailable than other Mg preparations in a randomised, double-blind study." *Magnesium Research* 16(3):183-91.

Walravens, P.A., K.M. Hambidge, and D.M. Koepfer. 1989. "Zinc supplementation in infants with a nutritional pattern of failure to thrive: a double-blind, controlled study." *Pediatrics* 83(4):532-38.

Yehuda S., S. Rabinovitz, and D. Mostofsky. 2006. "Nutritional Deficiencies in Learning and Cognition." *Journal of Pediatric Gastroenterology and Nutrition* 43(S3): S22-S25.

Zhang, J. and R.R. Watson. 2002. "Health effects of docosahexanoic acid (DHA)--enriched eggs." R.R. Watson, ed., *Eggs in Health Promotion*. Ames: Iowa State Press.

Zimmermann, M.B. 2006. "The influence of iron status on iodine utilization and thyroid function." *Annual Reviews of Nutrition* 26:367-89.

Zoppi, F. and C. Cristalli. 1998. "Ionized magnesium in serum and ultrafiltrate: pH and bicarbonate effect on measurements with the AVL 988-4 electrolyte analyzer." *Clinical Chemistry* 44(3):668-71.

Index

Amanda Rose, PhD, is a social science researcher, a food politics writer, and a third-generation sufferer of postpartum depression. She writes on the Rebuild from Depression blog regularly about her efforts to stay out of the abyss. She lives with her husband, son, and mother in California's Sequoia National Forest.

Annell Adams, MD, is a board certified psychiatrist with a special interest in women's mental health and alternative treatments in psychiatry. With a BS in Nutrition, Dr. Adams consults with other physicians and therapists about the role of nutrition in depression during pregnancy and postpartum. She has made television appearances as an expert on depression in women. While balancing a clinical practice and three children, she also enjoys giving seminars to health care professionals on depression and the interplay of nutrition and alternative therapies in psychiatry. She can be found at the Gundersen Lutheran Medical Center in La Crosse, Wisconsin.

Jeanie Rose is an avid cook, gardener, and second-generation sufferer of postpartum depression. Jeanie began cooking at the age of ten. She founded an organic herb business in the 1970s and designed herbal teas. In the 1980s and 1990s, she operated the Emmaus House kitchen in California Hot Springs, known for gourmet menus on a shoestring. She contributes recipes and cooking videos to the Rebuild from Depression blog.

www.rebuild-from-depression.com